DOCTOR CHEKHOV

Chekhov in his Yalta garden 1901.

DOCTOR CHEKHOV

A Study in Literature and Medicine

by
John Coope

PUBLISHED BY CROSS PUBLISHING
CHALE, ISLE OF WIGHT

First published in 1997

© John Coope 1997

British Library Cataloguing in Publication Data

A catalogue record for this book is available from the British Library

ISBN 1 873295 21 9

Published and designed by Cross Publishing, Chale, Isle of Wight. England

Printed in Great Britain by The Bath Press, Bath

Contents

Acknowledgments

I owe a debt of gratitude to Kathleen Swift, my sister, who not only shares my enthusiasm for Chekhov, but has translated many of the Russian texts. For further translations I must thank Elsa Baruch and Olga Villiers Kapnist and I am grateful to the latter for pointing out many mistakes in my references to nineteenth century Russia. Where I have quoted from the stories or plays I have used the excellent translations of Ronald Hingley in the *Oxford Chekhov*. For some of the letters I have used the translations of Simon Karlinsky and Henry Heim[1] and for others those of Avrahm Yarmolinsky[2]. In the chapter on the journey to Sakhalin I have quoted from *The Island. A Journey to Sakhalin* by Luba and Michael Terpak published by Century.[3] Dr Julian Tudor Hart and Dr Eoin O'Brien gave me valuable advice on the manuscript. Lastly I must thank my wife Jean for forbearance and encouragement in generous amounts as required.

[1] *Anton Chekhov's Life and Thought*. Simon Karlinsky and Henry Heim. University of California Press. 1975.
[2] *Letters of Anton Chekhov*. Avrahm Yarmolinsky. Jonathan Cape. 1974.
[3] A. Chekhov. *The Island. A Journey to Sakhalin*. Translated by Luba and Michael Terpak. Century. 1987.

List of Illustrations

CREDITS

SCR Photo Library 1, 5, 6, 7, 8, 9, 16, 18, 19, 21, 22, 24, 25
Novosti (London) 3, 17, 23, 26
Mary Evans Picture Library 15
YIVO. Institute for Jewish Research (NewYork) 12

CHAPTER I

Introduction

Medicine is my legal wife, literature my mistress. When I'm bored with one I spend the night with the other. This is irregular but at least not monotonous and neither suffers from my infidelity. If I did not practice medicine, I could not devote my freedom of mind and my stray thoughts to literature. Chekhov

Medicine stands in his way. He would be a much finer writer if he hadn't been a doctor. Tolstoy

This book is the outcome of a literary pilgrimage, perhaps an obsession, which has engaged me off and on for many years in the intervals of my work as a GP in the north of England. My love of the theatre had early introduced me to Chekhov's major plays but it was only gradually that the shy but captivating author of these masterpieces came through to me and it was then that I realised how much Chekhov's career as a doctor meant to him and how the preoccupations of his clinical work had woven their way into his literary output.

The summer of 1977 found my wife Jean and myself tramping the grey streets of Moscow in search of Doctor Chekhov. Brezhnev was then in the ascendant and large posters announced the sixtieth anniversary of the revolution. We had joined a tour that included Moscow and Yalta which I foolishly presumed would allow us to visit his first house in Sadovy - Kudrinsky Street, the country estate at Melikhova and his last home in Yalta. In order to smooth the way I had asked The Society for Cultural Relations with the USSR in London to obtain a suitable introduction for us whilst we were in Moscow.

All this optimism took no account of the many headed bureaucracy that shields the Russian soul. I asked the lady behind the desk at the aptly named 'bureau' of the Ukraine Hotel how we could get to Melikhova.

Chekhov's 'chest of drawers' - his house in Sadovy - Kudrinsky Street.

She looked puzzled and said it was not a recognised tour. I pointed out that my guide book described it as a national museum. Changing tack, she then said there was no transport available. But, I insisted, the nearest railway station to Melikhova, Chekhova, is on the main railway line from Moscow. I could get a taxi from there. 'You are not allowed to go there without a permit'. 'Where can I get a permit?' 'The office is closed until next Monday'. Checkmate!

We gave up and went to look for the Moscow house in which he had seen his patients. It was a charming two storied building in brick with two bays facing the street, a steep copper roof with dormers, giving an air of bourgeois domesticity. I remembered that Chekhov had called it his 'chest of drawers'. After risking the Moscow traffic to take a photograph, we approached nearer to find a large notice on the door with the solitary word 'remont', 'under repair'. It was a word that we were to meet again when we at last found the house that Chekhov built for himself in Yalta. The whole of Russia seemed to be under repair with no fixed date for its completion.

The next day I went to the Lenin Library and, with the help of a postgraduate student, a lively girl who was studying Iris Murdoch, succeeded in threading the labyrinth of its protocol and obtaining some photocopies about Chekhov's early medical career. When I got back to the hotel Jean told me that my contact with the Society for Cultural Relations had at last born fruit. I rang back but the lady on the other end said that the doctors had now gone away to their dashas for the weekend. They were so sorry not to meet me. Another trail had run dry.

Exploring Chekhov's writings, however, was an altogether happier affair. In contrast to Dostoyevsky and Tolstoy, he made no claim to address the great problems of life or to promote some great synoptic vision of his own. Compared with *The Idiot* and *War and Peace*, large novels with what E.M. Forster termed a 'prophetic' agenda, the four plays and sixty stories of his mature years are domestic and muted making little attempt to impose an authorial view on the reader. Indeed, the absence of a high moral tone was regarded as a puzzling defect by some of his contemporaries. Like Jane Austen, Chekhov's attitude to life emerges indirectly, ironically in the course of his narrative.

He was soon recognised as one of the great masters of Russian prose. 'Together with Pushkin and Turgenyev,' said Gorki 'Chekhov created the Russian literary language'.[1] But the appeal of his writings does not seem to have been restricted by national boundaries. Since the early translations by Constance Garnett his works have had a particular attraction for English readers. Virginia Woolf was an early admirer. Responding to the stories, she wrote in 1925:

> the method which at first seemed so casual, inconclusive and occupied with trifles, now appears the result of an exquisite, original and fastidious taste, choosing boldly, arranging infallibly, and controlled by an honesty for which we can find no match.[2]

As for the plays, productions follow one another with a regularity rivalling that of Shakespeare and with an enduring fascination for producers, actors and audiences.

Critics have been much divided on the nature of his genius. Since 1917 Russian studies have tried to relate his writings to the social conditions and ideological struggles in his native country, pointing to the need for revolutionary change. Lenin was said to have been profoundly moved by the story *Ward Number 6* with its implicit condemnation of nihilism.[3] For others, Chekhov's writings are seen as the culmination of a tradition of realism that had its roots in Flaubert, Zola and Maupassant.[4]

---

[1] V.V. Khizhniakov. *Anton Pavlovich Chekhov Kak Vrach*. Moscow 1947. p.42.

[2] Virginia Woolf. *The Russian Point of View* reprinted in Collected Essays Vol.1 pp.238-246.

[3] A.I. Ulanova-Elizarovna. *Reminiscences about Illyich* 2nd Edition. Moscow 1930. pp.33-41.

[4] Leonid Grossman.*The Naturalism of Chekhov*. Translated in *Chekhov, a Collection of Critical Essays*. Ed. Robert Louis Jackson. Prentice-Hall Inc. 1967.

For still others the essence of Chekhov's art is the evocation of mood, often a twilight or autumnal one,[5] making him into an exquisite Russian impressionist. Directors and critics cannot agree on whether the plays should be regarded as tragedies or comedies, an argument that has continued since the days of Stanislavsky and the Moscow Arts Theatre, and is still not resolved. Indeed, one of the curiosities, perhaps one of the strengths of his writings is that they seem to evoke as many views as there are interpreters, giving them a fascinating ambiguity, holding a mirror up, as it were, to the reader.

Oliver Elton in his 1927 Taylorian lecture was, I think, the first English commentator to draw attention to what he termed a 'clinical' feel to his characterisation [6] and the description has been adopted, amongst others, by Ronald Hingley, the editor of the *Oxford Chekhov* and the author of the definitive English biography,[7] and, recently by V.S. Pritchett.[8] There is an obvious sense in which some of the stories might be called 'clinical', that is when they include a description of some specific mental or physical condition, such as the acute anxiety state of the student in the story *A Seizure* or the pains of childbirth in *The Party*. If one looks however through the whole body of his output the influence of his medical habit of mind can be felt on many occasions. It is not only that doctors and their patients appear frequently, but that the attitude that is revealed in the author is one of a balance between curiosity and compassion that is one of the virtues of a good doctor. Chekhov not only practised medicine throughout most of his adult life, but he was also convinced of the important part that it played in his literary output. Four years before he died he wrote to Grigory Rossolimo, professor of neuropathology at Moscow Medical School:

> My medical studies have had a serious effect on my writing. They have taught me the art of how to classify my observations and they have enriched my knowledge. The true worth of such knowledge for me as a writer could only be understood by those who are doctors themselves. Acquaintance with the natural sciences, with scientific method, has always made me guarded in my beliefs and

---

[5] Princess Nina Andronikova Toumanova. *Anton Chekhov. The Voice of Twilight Russia.* Columbia University Press. 1960.

[6] Oliver Elton. *Chekhov. The Taylorian Lecture.* Oxford. 1929.

[7] Ronald Hingley. *A New Life Of Chekhov.* Oxford. 1976.

[8] V.S. Pritchett. *Chekhov - A Spirit Set Free.* Hodder and Stoughton. 1988.

I have tried to conform with scientific facts where this was possible, and where this was not possible, not to write anything at all.[9]

Replying to his friend Alexei Suvorin who had attributed the opinions of the professor in *A Dreary Story* to him, Chekhov wrote:

The substance of these opinions is of no value to me as an author. They must be examined like objects, like symptoms, with perfect objectivity and without any attempt to agree with them or call them into question. If I had described St Vitus' dance you wouldn't expect me to consider it from the point of view of a choreographer would you?[10]

Maxim Kovalevsky, who was professor of history at Moscow and who knew Chekhov well wrote of him:

If fate had not given Chekhov artistic talent, he would have obtained fame as a scientist and doctor. His inclination was for exact sciences and in his literary work there appeared a rare phenomenon, an aptitude for objective analysis, which refused to compromise with any sentimentality or exaggeration.

The following chapters are, therefore, an attempt to see Chekhov from the point of view of his medical career and to discuss the impact of this on his literary output. I would not like to imply, even to the extent that Chekhov does in the above quotation, that 'facts' medical or otherwise, bear any simple relation to literary merit although it may illuminate his work to remember that he *did* hold these opinions. Nor, conversely, would I regard it as profitable to use the writings as a sort of quarry for historical or psychological material. The plays and stories must stand on their own, as they undoubtedly do. There is perhaps room however, for speculation about the mysterious relationship of science and art, and how they both illuminate in different ways the nature of human life. Chekhov, as a practitioner in both spheres, was undoubtedly interested in this relationship.

---

[9] A. Chekhov. Letter to Grigory Rossolimo. October 11 1899.
[10] A. Chekhov. Letter to A.S. Suvorin. October 17 1889.

Clinical medicine deals with the application of scientific knowledge to the manifold complexities of human lives. Today the doctor is urged to practice 'evidence based medicine' which requires an acquaintance with the increasing knowledge base of clinical trials which assess the risks and benefits of applying ever more complex technologies, and also an ability to explain these matters in terms that patients can understand. But this is not enough. Such knowledge is in the form of generalisations from studied populations. Practising medicine also demands an awareness of, and a sensitivity to the life situations of the individual patients, their framework of values and the astonishing range of human idiosyncracy. He needs to be able to identify with a great variety of people, to elicit what brings them for help as well as the values and expectations that govern their activities. Insights such as these are those required of a biographer or a writer of fiction and developing them is increasingly acknowledged in the training of medical students. Chekhov would have appreciated the emphasis now placed on the narrative structure of medical knowledge in a recent series of papers in the *Lancet* on *Medicine and Literature* [11] and the arguments presented by the American writer Katherine Montgomery Hunter in her perceptive book *Doctors' Stories*.[12]

In placing Chekhov in his medical context I have explored the position and expectations of a doctor in late nineteenth century Russia, the influence of his teachers and the whole zemstvo movement which involved taking medicine to the rural peasants. The zemstvo were district councils. They had been set up in the sixties during the reign of Czar Nicholas II as part of the package of liberal reforms that also included the abolition of serfdom. Although not envisaged at this time as a vehicle for medical services, this aspect of their work became dominant towards the end of the century and Chekhov took an active part in the zemstvo measures to deal with the cholera epidemics of 1891 and 1892.

Russian medicine, then as now, laid great emphasis on the social causation of disease, so it is not surprising to find him as a doctor being involved in relief work during the famine, in building schools or exploring the impact of penal settlements, the object of his monumental journey to Sakhalin. He also lived through times of accelerating and startling changes in medical science. The years before his entry into medical school had seen Lister's discovery of antisepsis, and this, along with the

---

[11] M. Faith McLellan/A Hudson Jones. The *Lancet* (1966) 348 109-11 and 734-36.

[12] Kathryn Montgomery Hunter. *Doctors' Stories*. The narrative structure of medical knowledge. Princeton University Press 1991.

introduction of anaesthetics had ushered in a revolution in surgery, bringing the possibility of treatment to many hitherto incurable conditions. Robert Koch's work on the bacterial cause of such illnesses as cholera and tuberculosis was throwing light on the causation of infectious diseases. At last, the scientific revolution which had started two centuries previously was beginning to have an impact on human suffering. Chekhov took great interest and a considerable pride in these achievements of medicine and would contrast them with the uninspired literary output of his day.

Several studies in Russian have dealt with Chekhov as a doctor. In particular V. V. Khizhniakov's *Anton Pavlovich Chekhov kak Vrach*,[13] I.M. Geyzer's *Chekhov i Meditsina*[14] and E.B. Meve's *Meditzina v Tvorchestvo i Zhizni A.P. Chekhov*.[15] Khizhniakov is factual and very thorough but does not try to relate Chekhov the physician to his literary works. Meve and Geyzer have strong idealogical overtones, lamenting the fact that Chekhov did not survive to see the 'new' Russia for which he had longed so passionately! Two short works in French should also be mentioned : *Antoine Tchekhov: Le Médecin et l'Écrivain* by Henri Bernard Duclos[16] and a thesis from Toulouse University : *Malades et Médecins dans l'Oeuvre de Tchekhov* by Marie Claude Chabrol.[17] Among background works that I have found particularly useful are *Doctors and the Administration of Russian Zemstvo Medicine : The Province of Moscow* by Peter Krug, an MD thesis from Wisconsin University, 1974,[18] and Nancy Frieden's *Russian Physicians in an Era of Reform and Revolution*.[19]

---

[13] V.V. Khizniakov. *Anton Pavlovich Chekhov kak Vrach*. Moscow 1947.

[14] I.M. Geyzer. *Chekhov i Meditsina*. Moscow. 1954.

[15] E.B. Meve. *Meditzina v Tvorchestvo i Zhizni A.P. Chekhov*. Moscow.

[16] Henri Bernard Duclos. *Antoine Tchekhov: Le Médecin et l'Écrivain*. Paris 1927.

[17] Marie Claude Chabrol. *Malades et Médecins dans l'Oeuvre de Tchekhov*. Toulouse University. 1963.

[18] Peter Krug. *Doctors and the Administration of Russian Zemstvo Medicine : The Province of Moscow*. 1864-85. Wisconsin University. 1974.

[19] N.H. Frieden. *Russian Physicians in an Era of Reform and Revolution*. Princeton University Press. 1981.

Portrait by the artist Nicholas Chekhov (1858-89) of
his brother Anton, 1883.

CHAPTER II

University Years

Chekhov entered the Medical Faculty at Moscow University in September 1879. The timing was fortunate as the late seventies and eighties were years of great achievement for the Moscow Medical School. A series of brilliant physicians and teachers led by the professor of medicine Grigory Zakharin (1829-97) had brought the practice and teaching of medicine to a new level of excellence. Discoveries in the science of medicine were not only bringing relief to many hitherto incurable diseases but gave renewed hope to the teachers and increased respect and authority for the profession. Twenty years previously things had been very different. According to Sergei Botkin (1832-89), perhaps the greatest of the Russian physicians in the nineteenth century, the teaching at Moscow in the fifties had been derisory with little or nothing in the way of practical experience. Most of the professors had completed their medical education abroad and merely read off in a perfunctory fashion lectures written sometimes ten or fifteen years previously. 'Our future' he says 'was ruined by our teachers who conveyed knowledge in the form of categorical verities without giving any incentive to original investigation'.[1] The status of the profession and the level of recruitment had sunk so alarmingly that in 1876 the government brought in an act which, among other measures, increased markedly the number of government scholarships for medical students.[2] As a result of this law there was an immediate rise in the number and quality of medical students which was sustained to the end of the century. Among this wave of new candidates was Anton Pavlovich Chekhov, then aged nineteen, having arrived in the capital only a few days previously from the small town of Taganrog in the far south of Russia. His father came from a

---

[1] I.M. Geyzer *op.cit.*
[2] N. Frieden *op.cit.* p.47.

peasant family and had run a grocery business until incompetence led to his bankruptcy, and the family had moved to Moscow the previous year in search of employment leaving Anton at home to finish his education. He was the third of six children and, with the failure of the breadwinner, his mother looked to the older boys to help keep the family afloat. Chekhov's two older brothers Alexander and Nicholas however, although gifted, were drifters and alcoholics. His mother wrote to him in February in a tone of desperation.

> Come and join us soon. I can hardly wait. And if you take my advice apply to the Medical School. Medicine is the best career. Remember, Antosha, if you work hard you will be always able to earn a living in Moscow.[3]

His mother's wish may have influenced his choice of medicine although he seems to have been thinking along these lines since a severe attack of peritonitis at the age of fifteen.

During his years at Moscow University he lived with his family in a series of tenements in an area of the city crowded with brothels and cheap students' lodgings. His mother took in two other medical students in addition to her large family and Chekhov found himself one of ten people living in four rooms. The first view of the university was somewhat dispiriting to him, if the student's introduction to the university in *A Dreary Story* is drawn from his own experience.

> Now come the gloomy university gates so long in need of repair, the bored janitor in his sheepskin coat. On a bright boy fresh from the provinces with the idea that a temple of learning really is a temple, such gates cannot produce a salutory impression. By and large the university's dilapidated buildings, its gloomy corridors and grimy walls, the dearth of light, the melancholy vista of steps, coathooks and benches have played an outstanding part as a conditioning factor in the history of Russian pessimism.

A more cheerful description is given by a doctor who recounted his experiences as a Moscow medical student at about the same time.

---

[3] E.J. Simmons. *Chekhov : a biography*. University of Chicago Press 1962.

Moscow University Medical School.

The medical students' quarters were rows of white single storied houses. At each half hour of the day a huge bell rang out. Little yellow pony traps passed rattling down the street and disappeared under ancient trees. As darkness fell, yellow oil lamps were lit and the shouts of students were to be heard from the direction of the town. The students were dressed in dark green officers' coats with gold buttons and fur caps lined with blue. As they came in from visiting the theatre, an hour and a half's walk away, they would be singing gaily. In the morning at eight o'clock exactly there would be the sound of carriages and horses as the teachers of the medical faculty went out to their clinics. They emerged at two hour intervals through the day, at first the physicians then the surgeons and finally the other specialist departments. In winter, instead of horse drawn carriages they would travel in sledges. Moscow traditions gave additional status to the professors by allowing them to travel in style to their clinics. The less fortunate went on horseback or even on foot.[4]

---

[4] A.S. Abraham. *In Moscovsky Universitet. 1755-1930.* Yubileyny Sbornik. Paris 1930.

The curriculum of all the medical schools in Russia was regulated by the government under a law of 1838 which prescribed a five year course of study leading to the diploma of 'lekar' or physician.[5] The subjects were laid down by statute, and the state expected doctors who had qualified with the aid of a scholarship to enter government service, at least for a time, after graduation. Relations between the Ministry of Education and the universities, however, particularly the medical schools, were in a state of endemic conflict and this was to turn into open confrontation with the growing political unrest later in the century.

Chekhov had a state scholarship of three hundred roubles a year, from which he had to pay an enrolment charge to the university and fees to the professors as well as providing for his food and lodgings. In fact most of the instalment with which he arrived from Taganrog was promptly absorbed in settling household debts. It was this acute poverty that led him to turn his hand to writing to supplement the family income, and throughout his university years he submitted many stories to popular magazines such as *Splinters* and *Light and Shadow* that sold widely in Moscow. Already his mastery of descriptive writing and sensitivity to the varieties of human experience as well as an ever present sense of fun are evident in these comic sketches and he soon began to be noticed in Moscow literary circles.

There is comparatively little recorded about the progress of his medical studies. According to his friend and fellow student Grigory Rossolimo, who subsequently became a well-known professor of neuropathology at Moscow, he passed almost unrecognised among the other students on account of his exceptional shyness.[6] But he was certainly not simply there to get a degree and to do as little work as possible. Those who were near to him remembered a serious student immersed in reading the works of Darwen, Claude Bernard, Spenser and Buckle as well as standard medical texts.[7] He embarked on a number of projects that showed an interest in academic medicine unusual in a student: a *History of Authorities on Sex*, a study of *Women's Diseases* and a *History of Doctors' Work in Russia*. Materials assembled for the latter are still preserved in the documents relating to his student years. The list of one

[5] N. Frieden. *op.cit.* p.31.
[6] V.V. Khizniakov. *op.cit.* p.3.
[7] P. Bolkhovitinov, v V Viren : *Ogonyok*. 1944. Nos 25 & 26.

hundred and twelve references includes not only books on the subject but much primary source material, annals and reports of folk medicine.[8] It was evidently too large a task for a medical student and was left unfinished. Besides, he explained, he was becoming more interested as his course progressed in studying the living rather than the dead.

Considering his subsequent career it is perhaps not surprising that he was remembered as good at eliciting the patients' own accounts of their complaints. Rossolimo says :

> Chekhov did not go to work as an average medical student. He collected the elements of the case history together with surprising ease and accuracy.... But it was where one had to touch on the ordinary life of the patient, uncovering its intimate details, about how the illness developed into its present state that Chekhov seemed to bowl along effortlessly without forcing himself, in contrast to many students and even doctors who find it difficult to relate to the vivid statements emerging from the unique circumstances of patients' lives.[9]

In his relationship with the patients Chekhov became an enthusiastic disciple of Professor Zakharin and often referred to his influence after graduation. He wrote to a friend: 'How delighted I was to hear Zakharin's lectures' and later said to the editor Suvorin that he likened the professor to Tolstoy.[10] For Chekhov no praise could be greater than that. Zakharin laid emphasis on detailed history taking including precise analysis of the evolution of the presenting symptoms, the circumstances of personal life and occupation and the psychological state of the patient.[11] He was also a charismatic lecturer with an unforgettable style. In one term he devoted the first eight lectures to the description of a single patient, a tailor from Moscow with chronic abdominal pain. When Chekhov was a doctor he visited the university more than once to hear Zakharin lecture. Zakharin was also a convinced advocate of preventive medicine and Chekhov quotes his statement that

---

[8] E.B. Meve. *op.cit.* p.16.
[9] E.B. Meve. *op.cit.*
[10] V.V. Khizniakov. *op.cit.* p.35.
[11] E.B. Meve. *op.cit.* p.3.

the more experienced a doctor the better he knows the power of hygiene and the relative weakness of treatment. Only preventive medicine can hope to conquer disease in the population as a whole.[12]

After a brilliant career at the medical school his life ended in tragedy. During the last illness of Czar Alexander III in 1894 the story was put about that Zakharin, who was called to attend him, had administered poison to the patient and he was forced to resign his chair. In the riots that followed his home was torn down and his belongings burnt in the street.[13] There is no reason however to believe this paranoid rumour and Alexander III probably died of uraemia. The influence of Zakharin on Chekhov's attitude to life is obviously considerable and it may have helped to form the capacity for idiosyncratic observation of people that we find in his greatest plays and stories as well as the elimination of explicit moralising from his work, a feature that his contemporaries noticed, and which distinguished him from such writers as Tolstoy.

Grigory Zakharin professor of medicine at Moscow Medical School.

[12] A. Chekhov. Letter to A.S. Suvorin. 15th October 1884.
[13] F.N. Garrison. *Bull.* N.York. Acad. of Med. 1931. pp. 393-734.

The professor of public health was Eric Erismann (1842-1915) who was Swiss by birth and had done innovative work in St Petersburg on the influence of social conditions on health. He then went abroad to study under Pettenkofer in Austria before returning to Moscow as professor in 1875. Here he immediately undertook a monumental survey of factory conditions in the Moscow zemstvo which was published in 1881 whilst Chekhov was in his third year of studies. It was the first survey of its kind and did much to draw attention to the bad working conditions in the factories. Erismann became a moving force in the Pirogov Society, a medico-political organisation named after a great Russian surgeon. As this society became more politically active he became a marked man in government intelligence. In 1896 he espoused the cause of a group of women medical students who had been expelled from the university for political activity and was, like Zakharin, dismissed from his post.[14] Chekhov much admired Erismann's work and recommended him to the editor of the *Northern Herald* as 'a well informed, talented and a literary man'.[15] When he came to write his story *A Case History* in which he contrasted the luxurious life of the managers with the conditions of their workers he may have remembered the descriptions given by Erismann.

Yet another of Chekhov's professors is supposed to be portrayed in *A Dreary Story*. Despite its title there is nothing dreary about this story which is among his greatest masterpieces. It describes an old professor reminiscing about his life and the visitors that come to see him. His irascibility and intolerance are matched by a touching frankness about his own vulnerability and a consciousness of his imminent death. When he was asked by some students who the professor was meant to be, Chekhov said that the character was in part taken from that of a Professor Alexander Babukhin who had been appointed to the chair of histology four years before Chekhov came to the medical school. Babukhin was not only one of the finest scientists of his time but had the rare gift of being able to convey his enthusiasm to others. A contemporary recalls him as 'an outstanding lecturer, highly conscious of both the meaning of the story and his skill in giving an account of it'.[16] This certainly corresponds to the professor in the story who explains :

---

[14] I.V. Federov. A.B. Focht. Ob *A.P. Chekhovay Moskowkom Universitet.*
[15] I.V. Federov. *op.cit.*
[16] I.V. Federov. *op.cit.*

> No argument, no entertainment, no sport has ever given me such
> enjoyment as lecturing. Only when lecturing have I really been
> able to let myself go, appreciating that inspiration isn't an invention
> of the poets but really does exist.

Another admired lecturer in the medical faculty was Aleksei
Ostroumov, a popular figure with the students who made a courageous
stand on their behalf during the period of political unrest. Like Erismann
and Zakharin he was an advocate for a conspicuously social role for
medicine. He was much influenced by Charles Darwin and tried to apply
evolutionary principles to medical theory. Chekhov must have trusted
Ostroumov's clinical judgement because it was into his ward that he
chose to be admitted when his own health deteriorated.

Despite the political ferment of his years at the university, Chekhov
himself does not seem to have taken any active part in student politics.
There is no mention in his correspondence of the assassination of Czar
Alexander II that took place in Moscow when he was in his third year.
On one occasion however, when he was visiting the All Russian
Exhibition in 1883 he heard about a railway disaster that had just
occurred and mentioned to a friend with whom he was walking that such
an event could only take place in a swinish country like Russia.
Unfortunately the remark was picked up by a passing army general and
there was an uncomfortable few minutes whilst he was interrogated as
to what he meant. The incident, however, passed off with nothing worse
than a reprimand.

After his first year at the university Chekhov went south again to
Taganrog to settle some problems that had arisen over his scholarship.
He travelled with a student friend and they stayed at the summer house
of a family called the Zembulatovs. The two medical students enjoyed
showing off their newly discovered knowledge to the provincials,
dissecting rats and frogs in the garden or frightening the maids by placing
a human skull on a pile of books in their bedroom.

Working for his examinations or writing short stories was difficult in
the crowded circumstances of the family apartment. He confided to the
literary editor Nikolai Leykin:

> I write under the most abominable conditions. In front of me sits
> my non-literary work drumming away at my conscience. The
> child of a visiting relative is screaming in the next room. Nearby
> my father is reading aloud to my mother from *The Sealed Angel*

and someone has wound up the musical box and I can hear strains of La Belle Hélène. It makes me want to flee into the country. You can hardly imagine more difficult conditions for a writer. My bed is taken by a visiting relative who comes along now to ask my medical advice. 'My daughter must have colic to make her scream like that'. I have the misfortune of being a medical student and everyone thinks they can come and have a little chat about medicine. And when they are tired of medicine they want to talk about literature.[17]

Despite his protests, however, Chekhov was, like all medical students, proud to be able to show off his newly acquired knowledge. He wrote to his brother Alexander on the feeding of his infant daughter

You asked my advice about arrowroot. You have been waiting with understandable impatience for my reply and I am still silent. Please pardon me. I have been questioning the doctors, reading and taking thought and can conclude that nothing positive can be said about this flour. Some are against it. Others have no strong feelings either way. About one thing I can advise you. As soon as you see signs of diarrhoea, abandon it. In that case feed your 'fruit' on something else, for instance cow's milk with water. It is quite probable that there will be some diarrhoea in the summer. The mother is ailing. You're the one with the bottle. It is hot. The food is poor etc. but do not be chicken hearted. Diarrhoea like this can be cured by any old doctor. Decoct salep or an otvar of althaea, both with drops of opium. A poultice on the tummy. Don't give her porridge, bread, sunflower seeds, tea or hot drinks. If she asks for vodka don't give it to her. Spank her but do not give it to her. I'm off in a day or two to Voskresensk and from there I shall send you instructions how to feed, water, spank, care, what is important and what is not important, when to wean and when she should eat porridge and which doctor's prescriptions to avoid. All this is very important and I don't want to improvise without thinking it all out carefully first. It will all be based on the latest scientific evidence and will save you having to buy books on children's health and rearing that you fathers are so fond of. I will send all this soon on my word of honour and in reply you will send

---

[17] A. Chekhov. Letter to N.A. Leykin. August 1883.

me a hundred roubles and as many postage stamps as you can lay
your hands on.[18]

Salep is made from the dried tubers of orchidacious plants and althaea
is a preparation of the marshmallow root. Infusions of such substances
were often used for coughs, colds and diarrhoea. Or was it the drops of
opium that helped?

On another occasion one of his literary friends, Popudoglo, asked his
medical advice but this time the disease was more serious and eventually
proved fatal. Despite many different diagnoses Chekhov took a pride in
being the first to suggest his actual condition.

From his second year onwards Chekhov spent the summer vacation
working in the Chikino hospital at Voskresensk just south of Moscow as
an assistant to a Dr Pavel Archangelsky who subsequently gave an
interesting account of his clinical assistant.

The Chikino Hospital at Voskresensk where Chekhov worked as a student and after
qualifying in 1884.

---

[18] A. Chekhov. Letter to Alexander Chekhov.13 May 1883.

Anton Chekhov worked unhurriedly.   Sometimes a kind of hesitancy appeared in his manner but he did everything with attention and a manifest love of what he was doing especially towards the patients who passed through his hands. He listened quietly to them, never raising his voice however tired he was and even if the patient was talking about things quite irrelevent to his illness. The mental state of the patient interested him particularly. As well as traditional medicines he attached great significance to the effect that the doctor had on the psyche of the patient, and on his way of life.[19]

The country round the hospital where he went fishing or mushroom picking was a refreshing change from the city, and the evenings in Dr Archangelsky's house were occasions for discussions with the other students, readings from Nekrasov or singing popular songs. His brother Ivan was close at hand having taken the post of master at a nearby school.

In May 1884 Chekhov took his final exams and immediately returned to Voskresensk, this time with 'his doctor's passport' in his pocket, and stayed for a time at the New Jerusalem monastery before returning as a physician to the Chikino hospital. His first medical fees were for relieving a young woman of toothache, a monk from dysentery and for settling the stomach of a Moscow actress there on holiday. He wrote to Leykin :

> I was so astounded at the success of my new career that I gathered
> up all the roubles and sent them off to the Bannikov's Inn and got
> in exchange vodka, beer and such like medicines for my table.[20]

He was offered a position at Zvenigorod hospital about twenty miles to the south but turned this down, agreeing only to do a fortnight's locum there. Here he saw between twenty and thirty patients a day and experienced his first emergency operation. It was on a five year old boy with a paraphimosis. This is a condition in which the retracted foreskin becomes trapped behind the tip of the penis and one that requires considerable manual dexterity and experience to rectify. Unfortunately the child screamed so much and kicked his legs around that he had to

---

[19] E.B. Meve. *op.cit.* p.70.
[20] A. Chekhov. Letter to N.A. Leykin. July 23 1884.

admit defeat and send for a more experienced local doctor who relieved the patient and the perspiring young colleague.[21]   He also carried out medico-legal investigations, including post mortems and appeared in court in the role of a medical expert. He describes one such incident in another letter to Leykin :

> I made the examination, together with the local court doctor, in a field under the shelter of a young oak tree. The corpse was not known to be a man from a particular district, and the peasants, on whose ground the body had been found, prayed to heaven with tears in their eyes that he wouldn't dissect the body on their territory. 'The women and children will lie awake with fear.' The little village was up in arms - they were all there - the policeman with his badge, a widow, sobbing two hundred steps away from the place where the corpse was being opened up for examination and two muzhiks in the role of custodians standing by the body. Beside them flickered the dying embers of a small bonfire. The body, clad in a red shirt and new trousers was covered with a sheet. On top of the sheet a towel and an ikon. The examination showed twenty ribs to have been broken, oedema of the lungs and an alcoholic smell exuding from the stomach. It had been a violent death from suffocation. Pressure had been applied to the chest of the drunk man, pressure with something heavy, probably a hefty peasant's knee.[22]

In the autumn he returned to Moscow, put up his plate at the family house and waited for the patients to arrive. They were slow in coming and he found he was treating members of the family and impecunious literary friends that he did not care to charge.

> My medical career is coming on little by little. My family are having a good time of it. Even Feodossia Yakovlena comes to me for treatment. I treated Ivan the other day. It is a great luxury to have a doctor in the house.

One case that troubled his conscience was a family, the Yanovs, who

---

[21] R. Hingley. *op.cit.* p.50.
[22] A. Chekhov. Letter to N.A. Leykin. July 27 1884.

Chekhov's plate - 'Doctor A.P. Chekhov'.

developed typhoid fever, in the course of which illness the mother and one of the daughters died. According to his brother Michael, Chekhov was so shocked that he resolved for a time to give up medicine and devote himself to literature,[23] but the mood passed. The two Yanov sisters who survived became family friends. One of them embroidered an album cover for him with the words: 'In remembrance of saving me from typhoid fever' which is now displayed in the Chekhov museum in Yalta. He sandwiched his writing between professional duties.

> I started a story this morning. The idea I had for it was not bad but the pity of it was it had to be written in the gaps between other duties. After the first page Mrs. Dmitriev came in asking for a medical certificate. After the second page I received a telegram from Shekhtel saying he was ill so I had to go and see him. After the third page it was lunchtime and so on. And so I am writing in fits and starts, like an irregular pulse.[24]

By 1885 the flow of patients was gathering pace, but not his income, as he described in a letter to his Uncle Mitrofan.

> Medicine is beginning to come on. I'm working very hard all the

---

[23] M.P. Chekhov. *Vokrug Chekhova*. Moscow 1959. p.135.
[24] A. Chekhov. Letter to N.A. Leykin. 4 March 1886.

time. Every day I have to pay a rouble to the cabman. I've got a
lot of friends and not a few patients. I have to treat half of them free,
but the other half pay me in five and three rouble notes.[25]

There were moments of panic. One day he showed a patient to the
door and then suddenly remembered that he had made a mistake with the
dose on the prescription, putting the decimal point in the wrong place.
With the last money in his pocket he hired a carriage and set off in pursuit
of the patient recovering the prescription before it had been dispensed.[26]

In May of 1886 he went to stay with his friends the Kiselevs at their
estate at Babkino near to Voskresensk. He continued his medical
practice, however, from here, writing :

> I'm seeing a lot of patients, children with rickets and old folk with
> rashes. There's one old lady with erysipelas on her arm. I'm afraid
> that it will extend to cellulitis of the deeper tissues. There may be
> abcesses but I'm loth to use the scalpel on her.[27]

During the summers of 1888 and 1889 Chekhov rented a house for his
family near to the town of Sumi in the Ukraine. It was on the estate of
a remarkable family, the Lintvaryovs, with whom the Chekhovs became
very friendly. There was the mother, 'a kind plump old woman who
reads Schopenhauer and goes to church, but only to services honouring
her favourite saints', and three brilliant daughters two of whom were
doctors. The eldest of these had developed a brain tumour which had
made her completely blind but who bore the whole illness with remarkable
stoicism, laughing and joking with him and listening to him reading his
short stories. The second daughter was practicing as a country doctor and
Chekhov helped her with the surgeries.

> She is a quiet, shy, loving and homely creature. Patients are sheer
> agony for her and she is anxious about them to an almost insane
> degree. At our medical consultations we nearly always disagree;
> I bear glad tidings where she sees death; and I double the doses she
> prescribes. But, where death is evident and inevitable then my
> little doctor woman feels she's failed to come up to the mark as a

---

[25] A. Chekhov. 31 January 1885 - in Khizniakov *op.cit.*
[26] V.V. Khizniakov. *op.cit.*
[27] A. Chekhov. Letter to N.A. Leykin. 27 May 1886.

doctor. Once we took in a woman with a malignant tumour of the glands of the neck. It was so advanced that any sort of cure was out of the question. The patient felt no pain but it was certain that she would die within several months in dreadful anguish. My little lady doctor felt that she was in some way deeply to blame for this patient's condition, and concluded that all her medicine was useless.[28]

Meanwhile, in the intervals between patients, Chekhov continued to extend his literary career writing stories for the magazines and becoming increasingly recognised by the serious reading public. He pursued both his mistress, literature, and his legal wife, medicine, unwilling to leave either for the other. He had also completed and achieved a performance of his first full length play.

---

[28] A. Chekhov. Letter to A.S. Suvorin. 30 May 1888.

Poster advertising the first public performance of Chekhov's *Ivanov* on
19th November 1887 at Korsh's Theatre, Moscow.

CHAPTER III

Diseases of the Mind

The soul is ill; the soul is cured; the soul is not cured. Those are the emphatic points in his stories. Virginia Woolf

Chekhov's play *Ivanov* was written in the summer of 1887 whilst he was staying on the estate of the Kiselevs at Babkino. It was completed in just over two weeks in response to a request from the Moscow theatre manager, Fyodor Korsch who put it on at his theatre the same November. The opening night was a disaster. There was continuous brawling among the audience so that the police had to intervene and throw out the ringleaders. The actors did not know their lines and some of those playing minor parts were drunk. Even the prompter made mistakes. The critical notices on the following day were cool and one described the play as 'profoundly immoral'. It was not the sort of debut to encourage a budding dramatist of twenty-seven.

The subject was certainly unexpected for an author who, until now, had made a name for himself as a writer of humorous stories. Ivanov is a member of the gentry who has held a position of respect on the board of the zemstvo of his provincial town. His wife, Anna, has been declining for years with pulmonary tuberculosis. Although formerly a man of abundant energy and initiative, Ivanov's character has changed completely of late. In particular, he has become increasingly irritable with his wife for whom he no longer feels any love. Sasha, the daughter of a neighbouring landowner, becomes infatuated with him, and when Anna discovers them together she assumes that he has been unfaithful to her. This difficult situation is aggravated further by a brash young doctor straight out of medical school, Eugene Lvov, who takes Anna's part and berates Ivanov about his callous behaviour. In a furious outburst Ivanov reveals to his wife that she has not long to live. At the opening of the last act we hear that Anna has died and that Ivanov is betrothed to Sasha.

Preparations are being made for the wedding. Ivanov now decides that it would be folly to marry her and tries to withdraw. Sasha however will not hear of this and Doctor Lvov seizes the opportunity to humiliate Ivanov in public. In a final act of desperation he shoots himself.

The dénouement of the play is the least satisfactory part dramatically and Chekhov made several attempts to re-write it. In an earlier version Ivanov rather implausibly dies from shock on the stage. As a whole, however, it works very well in the theatre despite, or perhaps because of, the concentration of attention on the principal character. The pacing of the scenes, the economy with which the plot is unfolded and, above all, the verisimilitude of the dialogue are harbingers of the genius that Chekhov was to show in his later plays.

It is Ivanov's personality and his psychological malaise that are under scrutiny all the time, and these are described with a thoroughness and objectivity that reveal the clinician and the professional observer. If we take into account its brief gestation, there would seem to be every likelihood that this case study must have had its origins in his medical practice. Perhaps the insensitive Doctor Lvov is a critical reflection of Chekhov himself as a green and censorious young graduate. He was certainly capable of displaying righteous indignation at that time when writing to his dissolute elder brother Alexander.[1] Chekhov the dramatist however is the antithesis of this in his attitude to Ivanov which is compassionate but morally neutral. He wishes to exhibit a sick rather than an evil man. That in doing so he was contradicting the implicit assumptions of his time is neatly illustrated by the reaction of the director and actors to the play at the time of its first St Petersburg performance. They had been studying the play, and had come to the conclusion that Ivanov was, in his attitudes and actions, an unmitigated swine. Why then, did two sensible women fall in love with him? Should he not be given lines to alienate the sympathy of the audience? Whereas the idealistic Doctor Lvov should be portrayed to display clearly his heroic qualities. Having come to these crass conclusions they asked Suvorin to write to the author to persuade him to make the necessary alterations. Chekhov reacted angrily:

> If Ivanov emerges as a villain or odd-man-out and the doctor as a
> hero, if you can't see why Anna and Sasha can love Ivanov, the play
> clearly hasn't come off and there can be no question of staging it

---

[1] A. Chekhov. Letter to Alexander Chekhov. April 6 1886.

he writes to his friend Suvorin, the influential St Petersburg editor.[2]

He then gives a lengthy analysis of the play, describing the character of Ivanov as having followed the downward career of many prematurely weary middle-aged men in Russian society. Starting with great enthusiasm

> he's already bitten off more than he can chew - thrown himself into education, the peasant problem, scientific farming, the Herald of Europe, making speeches, writing to ministers, fighting evil, applauding virtue,

(the list would apply to Chekhov himself)

> but at the age of thirty or thirty-five he's already tired and bored. Ivanov does not understand the change that has overcome him, but it offends his sense of decency and leads to overpowering feelings of guilt. This guilt is a Russian feeling. A Russian always feels guilty when someone in his house dies or falls ill, and when he is owed - or owes - money.

Ivanov is always holding forth about his guilt. In act two he tells Sasha 'my conscience pains me night and day. I feel profoundly guilty, but I cannot understand of what'. Add to this the loneliness of his situation in society and the relentless demands of everyday problems and the downfall of our hero is inevitable. Then he describes the fluctuations in mood in such individuals as Ivanov.

> The susceptibility to depression (as Doctor Bertenson will explain to you) finds expression in more than merely whining or feeling bored. The life of the depressed man cannot be represented like this:

---

[2] A. Chekhov. Letter to A.S. Suvorin. December 30 1888.

It is not particularly even. The depressed do not lose their ability to work up a high pitch of excitement but their excitement lasts for a very short time and is followed by an even greater sense of apathy. Graphically it can be represented as follows:

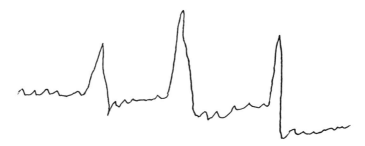

As you can see, the descent forms something rather different from a gradually inclined plane.

Chekhov now turns his attention to the character of Doctor Lvov. He is

a model of the honest, straightforward, hot-headed but narrow-minded and limited man. It is about his kind that intelligent people say 'he's stupid, but his heart is in the right place'. Everything resembling breadth of vision or spontaneity is alien to Lvov. He's tendentiousness personified, a walking cliché. He looks at every phenomenon and person through narrow blinkers and his opinions are all prejudices. He's ready to worship anyone who shouts 'make way for honest labour, and anyone who does not do so is a blackguard'.

He concludes with characteristic modesty -

I failed in my attempt to write a play. It's a pity of course. Ivanov and Lvov seemed so alive in my imagination. I'm telling you the whole truth when I say that they weren't born in my head out of sea-foam, or from preconceived notions or intellectual presentations or by accident. They are the result of observing and studying life. They are still there in my mind and I feel I haven't lied a bit or exaggerated an iota, and if they come out lifeless and blurred on paper, the fault lies not in them, but in my inability to convey my thoughts. Apparently it is too early for me to undertake playwriting.

Looked at from the viewpoint of the psychiatric practice of today, Ivanov presents a picture characteristic of endogenous depression. This condition which has come to be regarded as a common 'disease' of middle-life is still the subject of controversy as to whether it forms a discrete entity or merges with other types of depressive reaction. It is called 'endogenous' because there are no outside factors, 'exogenous', that would explain the depressed mood. With the change of mood is associated a constellation of other symptoms, prominent amongst which are insomnia, sexual apathy and impotence, fatigue, irritability and loss of interest in usual pursuits. There is often a feeling of unreasonable guilt and the condition carries a considerable risk of suicide. The response of these patients to mood-elevating drugs as well as some evidence of a biochemical abnormality in the brain resulting in low levels of certain amines point to this being a definable disease with an organic basis. It is also known that patients subject to swings of mood - so called cyclothymic individuals - are more prone to develop depressions of this kind.

Chekhov's description of Ivanov fits this clinical picture very accurately.

> I've become so irritable, hot tempered, rude and petty that I don't recognise myself,

Ivanov explains to Doctor Lvov in Act One,

> Every day I have a headache, I can't sleep, my ears are ringing, I have positively nowhere I can go, nowhere!

And, later in the same act he describes a loss of interest in his wife,

> the gist of it is, I was passionately in love with her when I married but.......five years have passed. She still loves me, but I! (helpless gesture with his hands). Here you are telling me that she'll die soon and I feel neither love nor pity. From someone else's view I must really seem terrible. I myself cannot understand what is happening.

He tells the fatuous Count Shabelsky not to snoop round when he is talking and immediately regrets hurting his feelings. The same sequence of irritability followed by guilt emerges in his reactions to his wife. 'How annoying you are! My God! What am I saying? Anna, I've been talking to you in an impossible tone. I've never been this way before.' Chekhov

was not content merely to describe the condition. He explicitly rejects
the naive interpretation of events put forward by the ingenuous Lvov.
'No, doctor' Ivanov says to him, 'each of us has too many wheels, screws
and valves to be judged by one another on first impressions or by two or
three external symptoms.' This agnostic approach to his subjects'
motivation is probably what shocked the critics on the occasions of the
first performance of the play and it still puzzles many interpreters of
Chekhov. Today it is a commonplace of medical practice to see depressed
patients in this way but it is an attitude that has only slowly emerged.

The first systematic studies of depressive illness were undertaken by
the French psychiatrists Falret and Baillarger working in the great
Parisian asylum of Salpêtrière during the first half of the nineteenth
century. Falret recognised cycles of elation and depression and described
them in a paper entitled *De la Folie Circulaire* published in 1854.[3]
Thereafter there were numerous descriptions of types of 'melancholia'
particularly the grosser disorders that led to patients being confined to
asylums. During Chekhov's undergraduate days the departments of
psychiatry and neuropathology at Moscow were united under a single
professor, Koshevnikov, who had done much to encourage the study of
both these disciplines in Russia. His most brilliant pupil, who later came
to occupy the chair, was Sergei Korsakov, whose name was to attain
general familiarity in medicine by becoming attached to a particular type
of dementia found in patients with alcoholism. Korsakov, who was well
known to Chekhov, was the first academic to give a course of lectures on
psychiatry in Moscow in 1887 and two volumes of his lectures were to
be found in Chekhov's library at Yalta. Here is Korsakov's description
ot the depressed patient.

> People in this state often say that they cannot understand how other
> people can approve of them; they think of their own past
> achievements as so many melancholy mistakes. The degree of
> such mood changes fluctuates, varying from mild downheartedness
> to the deepest despair and a degree of mental suffering that the
> patient can hardly live with and that drives him to suicide. In these
> states patients feel as if all their emotions are dulled. They cannot
> react normally - not only to love and happiness but even to anguish
> and sadness; so that they feel like wooden or stone monsters.[4]

---

[3] M. Falret. *De La Folie Circulaire*. Bulletin de l'Académie Médicale. Paris. 1854. Vol 19 p. 382.
[4] S. Korsakov. *Course of Psychiatry*. Moscow. 1901. 2nd Edition p. 250.

However, as Chekhov states in a letter to Suvorin, the characteristics of Ivanov's depression have not been drawn from textbooks but from close study of his patients. That the subject fascinated him is shown by his stating to the writer Yasinsky 'If I had not been a writer, I would probably have been a psychiatrist, but I would have been a third class psychiatrist and I preferred to be a first class writer.'[5]

Melancholic and depressed characters appear with some frequency in the plays and stories. Voinitsky in *The Wood Demon*, his next play, who also shoots himself, is quite a different personality. Irascible and impotent by nature there is no evidence that he has ever been any different. His suicide is an act of desperation brought about by a chain of circumstances and is almost accidental. Indeed in Chekhov's transmutation of the play into *Uncle Vanya*, the suicide becomes an ineffectual attempt at murder, perhaps a gesture to attract attention to Vanya's unfortunate situation or a ploy designed to awaken sympathy from the women folk that abound in the house. When he states in the last act that 'I'm mad, irresponsible. I have the right to say silly things.' Astrov, the family doctor - and a near self-portrait of the author - retorts:

> That's an old trick. You're not mad. You're simply a crank. I used
> to think that every crank was sick or abnormal. But now I believe
> it's normal for a man to be a crank. You're perfectly normal.

Vanya is one of those people who never stop lamenting their unfortunate luck, how terrible life is, how unjustly they have been treated and so on, a state that is quite different from true depressive illness in that it seems to be a permanent characteristic of their personalities. They seem born with a grudge, a chip on the shoulder. Laevsky in the long story *The Duel* is of the same stamp as Vanya and it is the conflict between him and the extrovert and confident biologist Van Koren that precipitates the conflict in the story. These may be called constitutionally depressive characters. At the other end of the spectrum are those depressions that are precipitated by exposure to distressing circumstances. Two of Chekhov's stories describe 'exogenous' depressive attacks of this type. In *The Fit* a group of students pay a visit to the brothel district of Moscow. For two of them, the medical student and the arts student, the adventure is a light-hearted romp. They accept life as they find it, drink and enjoy themselves and do not notice the suffering that goes on round them. For the third student,

---

[5] Ieronim Yasinsky. *Novel of my life*. 1926. p. 268.

Vassiliev, however, from the law faculty, the experience is shattering. He is appalled at the paradoxes in commercial sexuality and cannot understand how people can come to accept such depraved values. When he returns to his room he finds that he cannot dismiss the plight of the exploited girls from his mind and feels an impulse to go and do something to help them, but the problem is evidently far too big for one individual to tackle and he relapses into a profound depression.

> When daylight came and the carts rattled on the streets, Vassiliev lay motionless on the sofa, staring at one point. He did not think any more of the women, or of the men or of the apostles. All his attention was fixed on the pain of his mind, which tormented him. It was a dull pain, indefinite, vague; it was like anguish and the most acute fear and despair. He could not say where the pain was. It was in his breast, under the heart; beneath this pain life seemed repulsive. The thesis, his brilliant work already written, the people he loved, the salvation of fallen women, all that which only yesterday he loved or was indifferent to, remembered now, irritated him in the same way as the noise of the carts, the running about of the porters and the daylight.

He stays in this helpless state neglecting his food and his appearance for some days until his friends, alarmed at the change in his condition, summon a doctor. 'Mikhail Sergevich, a stout doctor with fair hair' appears and immediately starts to question the patient.

> He asked whether Vassiliev's father had suffered from any peculiar diseases, if he had fits of drinking, was he distinguished by his severity or any other eccentricities? He asked the same questions about his grandmother, mother, sisters and brothers. Then he went on to ask Vassiliev whether he had any secret vices in his early youth, any blows on the head, any love passions, eccentricities or exceptional infatuations.

Such a catalogue illustrates well the presuppositions of late nineteenth century psychiatry. The fundamental cause of most mental disease was believed to lie in the constitution of the individual which was determined by hereditary traits and to be elucidated by genealogical investigation, which was enquired into meticulously and at length. Other factors such as emotional experiences, sexual indulgence and, particularly, masturbation, were calculated to enfeeble the nervous system, as were also head injuries. Once the ground was rendered fertile, as it were, by these predisposing factors, it only remained for some precipitating cause to bring about the nervous collapse.

In the story the doctor cannot find any particular cause and falls back on prescribing a potassium bromide mixture and some morphine, both central nervous system depressants, and the equivalent of today's ubiquitous tranquilizers. He disappears leaving Vassiliev wondering why he is dubbed a lunatic for being shocked by a truly shocking situation in the brothels. One feels that Chekhov sympathised with the 'patient' and has nothing but contempt for the inadequate and stereotyped approach of the doctor who merely applies his rules of thumb and dashes off a couple of prescriptions.

The Fit was written in 1888 as Chekhov's contribution to a memorial volume commemorating the death of the writer Vsevolod Mikhailovich Garshin. Garshin, who was Chekhov's senior by five years had suffered from recurrent depressive illness for many years and had eventually killed himself by jumping over the well of his stairs. As a youth he had gone to the rescue of a girl who was being dragged off by the police on a charge of prostitution - a fact that Chekhov commemorates in his story. Throughout his writing Garshin had shown a phenomenal sensitivity to suffering and injustice. When he heard of the thirty thousand Slavs who had been killed in the Russo-Turkish war the thought of those dead 'drove out' he said 'all other interest in life. I wanted to spit upon all your scientists and societies, if with all their theories, they cannot prevent such things happening.'[6] He intervened to try and prevent the execution of one of the assailants of the Grand Duke Nicholas in 1880 but after obtaining a promise that the student involved, Louis Melikov, would be reprieved he came across his body hanging from a public gallows. Such events plunged Garshin into a series of severe depressive states. We know that Chekhov was well aware of Garshin's illness and he acknowledges in a letter to another literary friend that his thoughts often reverted to the writer's mental affliction.[7]

Ten years later, Chekhov was to turn once more to the theme of an attack of depression in a young person in *A Case History*. A professor of medicine is asked to visit the daughter of a mill owner in a provincial town and, being unable to go at the time sends his house physician,

[6] E.B. Meve. *op. cit.* p. 47.
[7] A. Chekhov. Letter to A.N. Plescheyev. 18 September 1888.

Korolyov. When Korolyov arrives he is confronted on the doorstep by the mother, a widow, and by a loquacious and opinionated housekeeper who proceed to give him at length their half-digested medical theories as to why the daughter of the house, a girl of twenty, has become subject to attacks of weeping and palpitations. They have been up all the previous night, hovering round her bed and expecting her hourly demise. After a brief consultation with the girl herself Korolyov realizes that she is not physically ill but extremely depressed and anxious, that she needs 'not medicine or advice' but a few kind words, displaying the wisdom that the doctor in the previous story so conspicuously lacked. After reassuring the family, he is about to make his departure when the mother implores him to reassure them by staying overnight in the house. He reluctantly agrees and, after the evening meal he takes a stroll round the great factory that lies near by, and, as he does so, he remembers the faces of the mill workers seen from his carriage as he entered the town earlier that day. He is suddenly overwhelmed by the meaninglessness of the brutal slavery to which they are subjected and by the contrast between their lives and the food-loving housekeeper in the big house.

When he returns to his bedroom he hears his patient sobbing and goes into her room to try and comfort her. He persuades her to divulge her fears about her situation and her underlying loneliness and, as a human being rather than as a professional helper, extends a hand of friendship to her, showing that her loneliness and worries are natural and normal in a person in her position. By the time he leaves next morning, the young lady, dressed in a white frock and ribbon in his honour, is obviously feeling much improved. The young doctor here rejects the naive attempt to treat the psychological reaction as a disease by the patient's family. Like Vassiliev in *The Fit* the daughter of the house had a depressive reaction to external circumstances and was best 'treated' by enabling her to understand her own reactions. The more severe and 'endogenous' depressions like that of Ivanov were more difficult to manage. Indeed nothing could then be done to cure the condition at all. Chekhov's descriptions of these varieties of depression and their distinction from the constitutionally disaffected characters like Vanya and Laevsky is a remarkable achievement. These studies show how well he understood the spectrum of depressed behaviour and the reaction of doctors faced with such patients. In particular he emphasizes the dangers of 'snap judgements,' moralizing, and the ready resort to the prescription pad, features that are not completely absent today in our professional approach to depression.

The last half of the nineteenth century and the first half of this have been termed the 'Asylum Era' of psychiatry. They were times when large numbers of the insane poor for which little or no care had been available were collected together into large institutions like Colney Hatch in London. The provision of such custodial centres in Russia had been slower to develop than in many other European countries. The great distances involved and the primitive living conditions of the peasants, as well as the impoverished exchequer created huge obstacles to such services. Indeed, prior to the inauguration of the zemstvo in the early sixties, the severly incapacitated were left in their villages. If they were considered a danger to others, they were incarcerated in primitive establishments where they were huddled together, irrespective of diagnosis in conditions more akin to a prison. The zemstvo, having undertaken to provide the necessary medical services in the region for which they were responsible, were technically obliged to build asylums but lack of funds often made this impossible. In 1879 the Minister of the Interior issued an order authorizing the central government to pay fifty per cent of the cost of such buildings and a few were erected. Chekhov must have made a study of the subject for in 1888 he offered to contribute to Suvorin's *Russian Calendar*, a brief encyclopaedia, an article on 'Lunatic Asylums in Russia'.[8] One new building was the hospital at the village of Pokrovskoe, eleven miles from Chekhov's estate at Melikhova, where a psychiatrist friend Vladimir Yakovenko was superintendent. On 31st July 1892, we find him writing to Yakovenko

> I don't know if you take out-patients but all the same I am sending you the manufacturer Kochelkov who is an alcoholic factory owner. His complaint: 'I drink vodka and cannot stop.' I used the brief time at my disposal and prepared the background information about this patient, which I hope you will find useful.[9]

Yakovenko had done much to pioneer taking psychiatric help to the peasants. The year after this letter he was arranging a meeting of the zemstvo doctors of the Moscow district at his hospital and Chekhov certainly attended on this occasion. Such pioneering spirit was not universally apparent however, and Chekhov demonstrated the depths to

---

[8] A. Chekhov. Letter to A.S. Suvorin. 10 October 1888.
[9] A. Chekhov. Letter to V. Yakovenko. 31 July 1892.

which psychiatric care could sink in his celebrated story *Ward Number Six* which appeared in 1892.

The roof of the ward is rusty and the chimney half collapsed, the porch steps are rotted and overgrown with grass. Inside, conditions are much the same. The patients, dressed in navy-blue hospital smocks and nightcaps sit or lie on their beds in a filthy ward that smells like a zoo and are frightened and beaten into submission by a brutal attendant, Nikitka. The hospital, of which this is a neglected corner, is an old charitable institution and the zemstvo has taken no steps to open a new clinic in the town on the grounds that a hospital of sorts already exists. The medical superintendent, Ragin, is a sensitive and philosophic individual but he has come to adopt a completely passive and fatalistic approach to medicine, arguing that suffering and death are so much part of the human condition that it is vain to try and alter them. He does the minimum consistent with drawing his salary and spends the remainder of his afternoons in philosophical discussions with the postman. One day, Ragin, whilst passing the ward, is noticed by a patient who, not having seen the doctor for years, starts to shout abuse. He looks into the ward and enters into conversation with the patient, Gromov, an eccentric nobleman who was locked up many years ago suffering from delusions of persecution. He is amazed to discover that Gromov is, like himself, but unlike practically anyone else in this provincial town, interested in ideas and philosophic dilemmas. They strike up a friendship with the result that the staff and patients are treated to the strange sight of the medical superintendent making repeated visits to ward six where he is seen to be seated on the bed with one of the patients, both deep in conversation. Doubts of his sanity are circulated and these are reinforced by a new doctor who is transparently interested in succeeding to the senior post. The forces of authority inexorably close round the pathetic Ragin and, after an enforced holiday during which the administrative reins are whipped from his hands, he finds himself certified and incarcerated in his own ward where he dies of a stroke.

The story has the terrifying and claustrophobic quality of Kafka's *The Trial*. Ragin himself is certainly sensitive and interested, in a theoretical manner, in the progress of scientific knowledge.

> When he reads at nights, medicine moves him, arousing his admiration - his enthusiasm even. And in very truth, what a dazzling break-through! What a revolution! Thanks to antiseptics, operations are performed that the great Pirogov never dreamed of.

Ordinary doctors venture on operations on the knee joint, abdominal surgery produces only one fatality per hundred operations and stone matters so little that no one even bothers to write about it. There is radical treatment for syphilis. And there is the theory of heredity isn't there, and hypnotism? There are Pasteur's and Koch's discoveries, there are hygiene statistics, there's our Russian Rural Welfare Service. Psychiatry with its modern methods and classifying disorders, its techniques of diagnosis and treatment.....a gigantic stride forward that! The insane no longer have cold water poured over their heads, and they are not put in strait jackets, they even have theatrical performances and dances arranged for them - or so the newspapers say!

The catalogue gives us a bird's eye view of the growing points of medicine in the nineties and, despite the ironic clause, Ragin is obviously well informed and even enthusiastic about the progress being made. But he has succumbed to an indifference that was characteristic of the fatalism of some of Tolstoy's followers.

What does it all matter? There are antiseptics, there is Koch, there's Pasteur - yet the essence of things has not changed a bit, sickness and mortality still remain. People arrange dances and shows for lunatics, but they still don't let them loose. So it's all a snare and a delusion. Between the best Viennese clinic and my hospital there is no real difference at all.

One can imagine Ragin reacting with instinctive sympathy to the arguments of Ivan Illich in *Medical Nemesis*[10]. All this medical activity is very impressive but in the long run, does it bring all that many benefits? Ignoring or taking for granted the relief of pain and suffering brought about by say pain killing drugs, or operations for stone, these apologists of medical nihilism load the evidence against scientific medicine with stories of professional greed and incompetence or with nostrums about the inevitability or even the value of suffering. For reasons such as this Ragin does not feel inclined to put his knowledge into effect and the medical authorities who employ him have no interest whatsoever in the sufferings of patients and fill purely institutionalised roles. Between

---

[10] I. Illich. *Medical Nemesis; the expropriation of health*. Calder and Bogars. 1975.

these two poles of inaction the patients are slowly rotting in the ward. Lenin's reaction was understandable. 'When I finished reading the story yesterday' he said to Ulyanova Elizarovna 'I felt strange and could not stay in my room, so I got up and went out. I felt as if I was locked up in Ward 6'.[11] Psychiatry was, and is, the poor relation of other branches of medicine and Chekhov's story was a vigorous protest at this neglect on behalf of all the patients in all the psychiatric wards, undermanned, ill-cared for, brutally treated and unvisited by medical staff. It is a situation which still applies in many hospitals today, to our shame, where impoverished resources tend to force even well-meaning doctors into abandoning standards of care that they know to be desirable, and leave little time for the compassionate development of medical science.

Ward Number Six mentions psychotic patients but, apart from a brief description of the genesis of Gromov's delusions, Chekhov makes little attempt to probe the psychology of more severe psychoses. In 1894 however he embarked on just this task in *The Black Monk*. It is a story that has received a large and varied exegesis at the hands of Russian scholars.

The philosophy lecturer, Kovrin, feeling tired and overwrought goes to stay in the country with a tutor from his student days. The old man is a horticulturalist and shares Chekhov's passion for orchards. He has also an eligible daughter Tania with whom, in the idyllic setting of the country house, Kovrin falls in love. One evening he spins a tale to Tania about a monk that has appeared to a number of individuals in the past and explains the phenomenon by the laws of optics as a series of mirages, each derived from the preceding one. Towards sunset on the same day Kovrin is alone, walking in the estate when he sees a black shadow on the horizon, like a whirlwind, that approaches him at great speed. As it approaches it takes the form of a black monk. The apparition turns its pale face towards him as it passes and smiles before disappearing across the river. Instead of feeling frightened, Kovrin is strangely elated but considers it tactful to say nothing to his hosts regarding the apparition. A few days later the black monk again appears to him, this time in the garden, sits down by his side and engages him in conversation. The monk explains that Kovrin has a great destiny, that without men of genius of his sort mankind would soon perish, that he is ill because he has worked heroically and that the fact that he is mentally ill should not worry

---

[11] A.I. Ulanova Elizarovna. *Reminiscences about Illyich.* 2nd Edition. Moscow. 1930. pp. 35-41.

him for madness is a first cousin of genius. Kovrin rejoices to hear all this as it reflects and confirms his own beliefs. When the vision goes, he remains elated and determined to sacrifice his health and life for the benefit of mankind.

Kovrin marries Tania and takes her back to the town with him, but his life is more and more occupied with his recurrent hallucinations. One day Tania observes him talking to an empty chair and realises that he is ill. He is wrapped in a fur coat and shawl and driven to the doctors. When we see him again he is a changed man. His hair is cropped. His face is stouter and paler and he is no longer elated and enthusiastic. Tania is supervising the 'cure' and making sure that he takes his bromide and his milk. But he is depressed and irritable, resents her attentions and, to her distress, pours scorn on her father. In the course of the next year Kovrin is offered a professorship - but is now too ill to take it up. He has started to cough up blood and to experience great weakness and sleepiness. He abandons Tania and her father and goes to live with an older woman in Yalta. One day a letter arrives from his wife describing how her father has died, which fact she attributes to Kovrin's cruelty. He goes out on to the balcony looking out over the bay, and there he sees for a last time the vision of the black monk. 'Why did you not believe me?' the monk asks. 'If you had believed me when I told you that you were a genius, you would not have passed these two years so madly and miserably.' As he hears these words Kovrin puts his hand to his mouth and realizes that blood is pouring out. A few hours later his lifeless body is discovered on the balcony.

The germ of this story arose, according to Chekhov's brother Michael, in a dream that the author had when at Melikhova. When he refers to the story he calls it a case of mania grandosa - a descriptive term indicating an excitable abnormality of the nervous system characterised by delusions of grandeur. Such delusions were, and are, regarded as typical of general paralysis of the insane, one of the principal manifestations of tertiary syphylis and although many authorities recognised the association between a previous history of syphilis and the subsequent general paralysis it was not until 1905 when Wasserman introduced the serological test that the association could be shown to be more than coincidental. The coughing up of blood suggests that Kovrin was dying, not from syphilis, but pulmonary tuberculosis, a condition that Chekhov had ample reason for bearing in mind. The relationship between tuberculosis and mental disease is not often referred to today when uncontrolled infection with TB is uncommon. In the nineteenth century however, the association was well known and referred to in all the standard text-books. Tuke's *Dictionary of Psychological Medicine*, for instance, published in 1892 devotes eleven pages to the discussion of 'phthisical insanity'. The expert contributor, Sir T.S. Clouston, summarises the evidence for a distinct psychosis caused by tuberculosis and comes to the conclusion, on statistical grounds, that the simultaneous occurrence of these two conditions is not fortuitous. He describes the features of a psychosis which often anticipates the pulmonary symptoms and in which paranoid delusions and sometimes hallucinations occur. It would seem likely that Chekhov wished to portray such a condition in Kovrin. That the content of the hallucinations concerns the role of genius and, that hoary old myth much espoused by Russian writers such as Dostoyevsky, of the close links between genius and insanity, adds an ironic twist to the causative role of the bacillus and, incidentally, gives us some insight into Chekhov's own attitude to these mystical theories that were having a pseudo-scientific revival at the hands of Max Nordau and the Italian criminologist Cesare Lombroso. Such ideas were being promoted in Russia by the writer Mireskovsky who was known to be inimical to Chekhov.[12] The inexorable and destructive progress of Kovrin's disease, destructive not only of his own personality and moral sensitivity but also of his wife's happiness and his old tutor's life with the symbolic downfall of their orchard (as in *The Cherry Orchard*) is a tragedy of human disease, a dilemma that no amount of moral uplift or political change can counteract. It points to the necessity for scientific and medical discovery.

Of the literary value of *The Black Monk* there is perhaps some doubt. Judged by the high standards he set himself this is not the most successful of the stories, although, as always in his mature work, there are many exquisite moments such as the description of the lighting of fires in the orchard to protect the trees from night frosts. Perhaps Chekhov was not entirely happy dealing with the psychological effects of gross psychotic break-down. Somehow the hallucinations seem more like the appearance of a traditional ghost than a manifestation of brain dysfunction. It was obviously an experience that, unlike depression, he had not lived through himself and was therefore compelled to describe from the outside.

The attempt to transmute the actualities of human mental processes, both normal and pathological, into an artistically realised form, so that others could identify with his characters, was very much at the heart of Chekhov's purpose. He regarded his position in occupying a dual

---

[12] E.B.Meve. *op. cit.* Chapter 2.

vantage point, both doctor and writer, as a great assistance in this task. In a letter, drafted but never sent to the writer Gregorovitch he says:

> I remember having read two or three years ago some story by a French author who describes a minister's daughter and gives, unsuspectingly, a clinically accurate picture of hysteria. I thought then that the sensitivity of the artist may equal the knowledge of the scientist. Both have the same object, nature, and perhaps in time it will be possible for them to link together in a great and marvellous force which is at present hard to imagine.

Such a fusion of literature and science seems as far from realisation as ever in a society where C. P. Snow's *Two Cultures* characterises our intellectual climate. But it is hard to deny the potential of such a fusion of effort in the field of mental disease. Indeed the emergence of the psychoanalytical school and its various progeny is perhaps an attempt to combine such introspective understandings with scientific observation. Unfortunately, instead of bridging the gap, further divisions have emerged and the ensuing controversy has led to closed intellectual positions and the emergence of mutually incompatible concepts clothed in jargon-ridden language.

Isaiah Berlin, in an essay on the eighteenth century Neapolitan philosopher Giambatista Vico[13], describes a sense of knowing which is basic to humane studies and quite distinct from scientific or inductive knowledge, or from deductive (or hypothetico deductive) systems, and which Vico had fully described for the first time. We all use it, however, in everyday life

> when we know what it is like, for instance, to be poor, to fight for a cause, to belong to a nation, to feel nostalgia, terror, the omnipresence of a god, to understand a gesture, a work of art, a joke, a man's character, that one is transformed or lying to oneself.

Berlin goes on to describe its nature as follows:

> It is knowing founded on memory or imagination. It is not analysable except in terms of itself, nor can it be identified save by

---

[13] Isaiah Berlin. *Vico's Conception of Knowledge in Against the Current: Essays in the History of Ideas.* Clarendon Press. 1955.

examples, such as those adduced above. This is the sort of knowledge which participants in an activity claim to possess as against mere observers: the knowledge of the actors against that of the audience, of the 'inside' story as against that obtained from some 'outside' vantage point: knowledge by 'direct acquaintance' with my 'inner' states or by sympathetic insight into those of others, which may be obtained by a high degree of imaginative power; the knowledge that is involved when a work of the imagination or of social diagnosis or a work of scholarship or history is described not as correct or incorrect, skilful or inept, a success or a failure, but as profound or shallow, realistic or unrealistic, perceptive or stupid, alive or dead.

Berlin regards this type of knowledge, attained by sympathetic identification, by the intense use of the imagination, as essential to some kinds of historical understanding. But it is also much needed in the study of human psychology, whether normal or abnormal, and it is one of Chekhov's great merits as a writer that he possessed a supreme capacity for this kind of knowledge. Compared with empirical 'external' descriptions, it is, no doubt imprecise and impossible to quantify, and one would not wish to deny the importance for the advance of science of precise observation and measurement. Any attempt, however, to obtain a view of the workings of the human brain that fails to take into account such imaginative understanding is bound to be dangerously limited and partial in its scope. Perhaps further progress in psychiatry requires an acceptance of this dual approach and, as Chekhov suggests, an intellectual framework in which both types of knowledge can play their part.

CHAPTER IV

Sakhalin

In January 1890, Chekhov surprised relatives and friends by announcing that he intended to make a five thousand mile journey across Asiatic Russia to visit the penal island of Sakhalin. This mountainous island, six hundred miles in length, lies along the Pacific seaboard of Siberia and is flanked to the east by the icebound Sea of Okotsk. In most seasons Sakhalin is bathed in freezing fogs with a mean annual temperature of zero centigrade. Until early in the 19th century this inhospitable tract of land had been inhabited only by aboriginal tribes but in 1875, after a prolonged territorial dispute with Japan, it had been added to the Czar's empire. Prior to this settlement, however, the Russian government had been deporting convicts to the island in the hope of establishing a colony there, so ensuring territorial supremacy in the area.[1] This was the furthest stretch of the great Siberian exile system which had been in operation since the middle of the sixteenth century, continually expanding and looking for new regions to exploit. Chain-gangs of criminals and political prisoners, amounting it was said to twenty thousand a year were constantly marching eastward, stopping at night in miserable 'étapes' or wayside prisons on their way to some remote provincial town or the mines of Kara on the Mongolian frontier. Few returned. As in the days of the Gulag Archipelago, many writers and intellectuals whose crime it was to have challenged, if only by innuendo or association, the authority of the government found themselves in exile. Dostoyevsky had published an account of his detention in *The House of the Dead* and, in Chekhov's own day the story writer Korolenko, whom he had met in Moscow, had drawn on his own experience of exile in his writings. One of these described the adventures of prisoners escaping from Sakhalin.

---

[1] Yuri Semyonov. *Siberia, its Conquest and Development*. Translated from the German by J.R. Foster. London. Hollis and Carter. 1963. pp. 292-314.

Another account of the Siberian exile system was circulating in Russia at this time. George Kennan, a journalist writing for the *Century Magazine* of New York had just completed an epic journey accompanied by an artist called George Frost, during which they had managed to visit most of the prisons on the Siberian mainland and, still more remarkably, had talked to large numbers of the political exiles.[2] This unmasking of the situation in the Czar's prisons was not accomplished without severe hazards and privations, and their account of their exploits and the shifts to which they were forced makes very compelling reading. At one stage they smoothed over some rather ruffled officials by producing a banjo and giving lively renderings of plantation songs. Naturally enough, the dissemination of Kennan's book in Russia was not encouraged, but it was certainly being widely read and discussed at the time and we know that Chekhov had encountered it.

Stories such as these must have troubled the consciences of many liberal-minded Russians. But the obstacles in the way of doing anything to influence the situation were formidable. The autocratic government of Alexander III with its empty coffers and muscle-bound bureaucracies, was extremely suspicious of any attempt to point out the inadequacy of its policies. Moreover the huge distances involved and the perils of embarking on the Great Siberian Highway which, despite its name, was still little more than a dirt track for much of its length, subject to floods, bandits and wild animals, made travel hazardous, prolonged and expensive. The greater part of the journey had to be made in a four-wheeled springless carriage known as a tarantass in which the luggage was stowed in the bottom of the vehicle, followed by a layer of straw and lastly the traveller, who lay on top in a kind of leather envelope and was shaken unremittingly for days on end, bitten by fleas, cold and soaked to the skin until every bone in his body ached. Such ordeals would have daunted many a fit man. And Chekhov was not fit. Already he had started to experience a racking cough and had noticed blood in his sputum, early signs of tuberculosis from which he was to die fourteen years later.

No wonder then that his brother Michael thought he was joking when told of the projected journey. His friend, Suvorin, the editor of the St Petersburg Journal *New Time*, remonstrated that it would be a prodigious waste of effort. But Chekhov was not to be diverted. He wrote to Suvorin:

---

[2] George Kennan. *Siberia and the Exile System*. (2 Volumes). London. 1891.

Both of us are mistaken about Sakhalin, but you probably more
than I.....I want to write one hundred to two hundred pages and
thereby pay off some of my debt to medicine, towards which, as
you know, I have behaved just like a swine. Perhaps I shall not be
able to write anything; nevertheless the journey does not lose its
attractiveness for me; by reading, looking round and listening, I
shall get to know and learn a great deal. I haven't left yet but thanks
to the books that I have been obliged to read, I have learnt much
of what everyone should know under the pain of forty lashes of
which I was formerly ignorant...... You say, for instance, that
Sakhalin is of no use and no interest to anyone. But is that so?
Sakhalin can be of no use or interest only to a country that does not
exile thousands of people there and does not spend millions on it.
After Australia in the past, and Cayenne, Sakhalin is the only place
where one can study colonization by criminals. The whole of
Europe is interested in it but we have no interest in it? From the
books I have read it is clear that we have let millions of people rot
in prison, destroying them carelessly, without discussion,
barbarously; we drove people in chains through the cold across
thousands of versts, infected them with syphilis, depraved them,
perpetuated criminals and placed the blame for all this on red-
nosed prison warders. All civilized Europe knows that it is not the
warders who are to blame, but all of us, yet this is no concern of
ours, we are not interested.[3]

One of the motives behind his journey was evidently to discover the
truth behind these stories. His sister Marya who worshipped her brother
corroborates this:

at that time much was heard of the hard life of the convicts on the
island of Sakhalin. People protested and grumbled but that was all.
Nobody took any active steps. Anton Pavlovich could not rest
after he discovered that convicts suffered so terribly and he
decided to go and see for himself.

Unlike Kennan and Korolenko Chekhov showed little interest in the
fate of political exiles. Brother Michael attributed his concern over

---

[3] A. Chekhov. Letter to A.S. Suvorin. 9 March 1890.

prison conditions to the chance finding of a copy of the Russian penal code on a visit to his house the previous year.[4] Whatever the truth of this assertion, there is little doubt that Chekhov was fascinated by the central problem of penology, 'what should society do with its criminal fringe?', a question that we seem no nearer to answering than in his time. To make a contribution to the solution of this problem, then, and thus to repay his debt to medicine was one of his main motives for making the journey. It was to be a work of science, a permanent contribution to the alleviation of human misery and he hoped to submit it for a doctoral thesis at Moscow University. The connotations of 'medicine' in the 19th century were somewhat broader then we are accustomed to and the sociological and biological fringes of the subject were regarded as very much within the province of a doctor. In fact, the hiving-off of a large number of separate disciplines that has occured during the last fifty years and the consequent narrowing of focus that has overtaken medicine itself, might not have struck Chekhov as an unqualified advance.

Influences other than the purely scientific were however at work in his life. In June 1889 he had seen his artist brother, Nicholas, die from pulmonary tuberculosis after a long terminal illness. This was a profound shock to him, as it was the first death of a close relative and must have thrown an ominous shadow on his own prospects. With this *memento mori* came a weariness with the cultivated life of the two capitals and the soirées to which this young and much talked of writer constantly found himself invited. He needed something sterner. 'This journey' he wrote 'will be perpetual toil, physical and mental for six months and it is what I need to shake off my depression and laziness. One must keep in training.'[5]

He threw himself into the preparations with characteristic thoroughness, reading all he could lay his hands on; treatises on geology, botany, meteorolgy, ethnography and the laws and statutes relating to criminals.

> It's such painstaking work that I think I shall die of boredom and exhaustion before I ever reach Sakhalin. All day long I sit, read and take notes. In the head and on paper nothing but Sakhalin. Mania. Mania Sakhalinosa.[6]

---

[4] Michael Chekhov. *Vokrug Chekhova*. Moscow. 1959.
[5] A. Chekhov. Letter to A.S. Suvorin. March 9 1890.
[6] A. Chekhov. Letter to A. Pleshcheyev. 15 February 1890.

He sent his older brother Alexander and Marya off to the library to hunt up for further details. He wrote a letter to the Director of Prison Administration, a certain Galkin-Vrasky, couched in subservient language, requesting permission to visit the prisons on the island.

On the twenty-first of April he set out accompanied by his sister and a few friends and travelled by train from Moscow to Yaroslavl. From there he went on alone taking one boat down the Volga and another up the Karma, he crossed the great Ural range towards the end of the month and wrote to his sister from Ekaterinburg:

The Chekhov family and friends in Moscow before setting out for Sakhalin 1890.
Front row: Michael (his brother), and Chekhov.
Second row: Two friends, Marya (his sister), Chekhov's mother and a young friend.
Third row: a friend, Ivan (his brother), and his father.

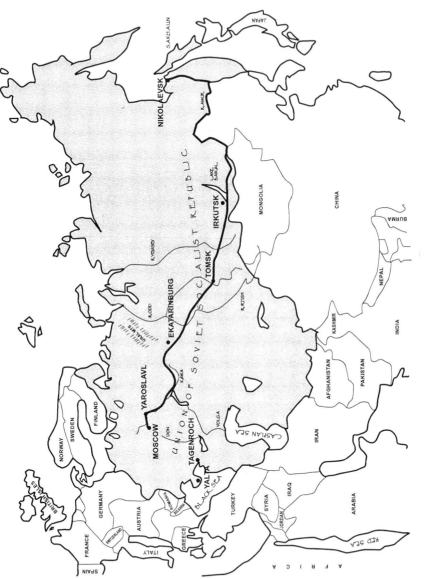

Chekhov's route through Siberia to Sakhalin.

The people here inspire the new arrival with a feeling akin to horror - they have prominent cheekbones, big brows, broad shoulders, tiny eyes and huge fists. They are born in the local cast-iron foundries and are brought into the world not by midwives but by smelters.[7]

From this point onwards the travel was by tarantass with all its attendant discomforts. He narrowly escaped death in an accident when his vehicle was run down by three troikas going in the opposite direction, their drivers asleep on the box. He was thrown to the ground with his luggage on top of him and all around the mangled vehicles, terrified horses and cursing drivers. Hardly had he recovered from this when news arrived of massive floods on the river Irtysh and before long he was having to dismount and lead the horses one by one through deep floods, a peasant testing the depth of the water in front of him with a stick.

> We're driving on. The felt boots are as wet as a latrine. They squelch, and my socks are like a sopping wet handkerchief that you've just blown your nose on after a heavy cold. The coachman is silent and clicks his tongue despondently. He would gladly turn back but it's too late. Darkness is falling.[8]

There were endless delays waiting for the ferries and he encountered further floods on the rivers Ob and Tom. On the evening of May 15 he arrived at Tomsk where he was entertained by the chief of police who thought of himself as a lover of literature, asked Chekhov for vodka, introduced him to his 'lady friend' - a married woman, read him a petition to the Czar in favour of divorce and finished the evening by taking him on a tour of local brothels. After a few days rest, Chekhov pressed on along the road to Irkutsk but his progress was constantly interrupted by the carriage breaking down, leaving him waiting for up to fifteen hours before it could be repaired. Despite his own problems, he kept a keen eye on the medical provisions made for the people in the areas through which he travelled.

> There are no hospitals and no doctors.
> The only people to treat the sick are male orderlies. Blood letting

---

[7] A. Chekhov. Letter to M.P. Chekhov. 29 April 1890.
[8] A. Chekhov. Letter to M.P. Chekhov. 16 May 1890.

with leeches and cupping there are, in huge brutal quantities. Once by the roadside I examined a Jew who was ill with cancer of the liver. He was exhausted and could scarcely breathe, but that didn't stop the district nurses from applying 12 huge blood-sucking leeches.[9]

This episode reminds one of the death of Chikildeyev, the waiter, in the story *Peasants*, after being cupped by a medical orderly. Chekhov regarded these unqualified practitioners with their cups and leeches, exciting the admiration of the credulous with their nostrums and apparatus, as dangerous impostors, doing more harm than good.

At length he reached Lake Baikal by steamer and from here he joined the course of the great river Amur on which he was carried by steamer for a thousand miles on its journey to Nikolaievsk on the Pacific, which he reached on July 5. The crossing of the Tartar Strait to Sakhalin was made on an ocean going vessel, the Baikal, which was carrying a detachment of soldiers to the island, together with a few convicts, one of whom was accompanied by his five year old daughter. His first sight of the island was not reassuring. Huge forest fires were pouring out black smoke. At Alexandrovsk, the chief town of Northern Sakhalin

> I could not see the wharf and buildings through the darkness and the smoke drifting across the sea, and could barely distinguish the dim lights at the post, two of which were red. The horrifying scene was compounded of darkness, silhouettes of mountains, and beyond the mountains, a red glow which rose to the sky, from remote fires. It seemed that all Sakhalin was in flames.

He took a cutter to the landing stage and went off in search of lodgings.

By a stroke of good fortune he ran across a junior doctor at the hospital who invited Chekhov to stay at his house and who turned out to be an unspoken critic of the administration and often presented petitions to the authorities on behalf of the convicts.

The following day Chekhov made a courtesy visit to the island's commandant. He found him in the midst of preparing for the quinquennial visit of the Governor General of Eastern Siberia. 'I'm glad you are staying with our enemy,' he remarked wryly. 'You will soon learn all our

---

[9] V.V. Khizniakov. *op. cit.*

Sakhalin Island.

little weaknesses.' It took Chekhov a while to accustom himself to the ubiquitous prisoners who crowded the streets and public places as well as being engaged in many service occupations. He awoke one morning about four o'clock to find a convict approaching his bed, on tiptoe, scarcely breathing. 'What's the matter? What do you want?' asked Chekhov nervously. 'To clean your shoes, your honour.' Next morning there was a ceremonial reception for the Governor General with a sung *Te Deum* and bands playing on the square. Many petitioners presented requests but he remarked that, out of ignorance, they often asked for something quite inappropriate that could easily have been granted by the local authorities. The governor must have been informed that a strange writer was on the island for he invited Chekhov to pay him a visit and questioned him closely on the purpose of his journey. He must have been satisfied for he gave Chekhov permission to visit all the parts of the island that he wished and to talk to any of the prisoners, except for those exiled for political offences. That evening the town was festooned with coloured lights and there were fireworks.

One of his first concerns was to find the printing shop of the police department and to arrange for the printing of data cards. These were, in

design, very like those used in population studies today. Each card referred to one household and contained on successive lines, the name of the settlement, the number of the house, the status of the person interviewed (convict, settler, peasant, etc.) surname and patronymic, other members of the household, age, religion, duration of residence, occupation, married status and, finally, whether the household was assisted financially by the prison authorities. Armed with these, he spent the next few months, starting at five o'clock every morning, making his way round the households accompanied by a solitary guard, barefoot and armed with a revolver, who carried his inkstand and often went ahead, hammering on the door to warn the inhabitants of the approach of the doctor and perhaps to give them his opinion of this strange enterprise. Considering the remoteness of many of the settlements and the virtual absence of roads on many parts of the island, it is an astonishing fact that he could claim to have interviewed every man, woman and child and completed over ten thousand of these data cards. They are still, I believe, extant in the Lenin Library in Moscow. It was the material contained in these cards that Chekhov was to use to form the scientific core of his book *Sakhalin Island* written in the years following his return.

He obtained a permit to visit the prison at Alexandrovsk which stood in the centre of the town and consisted of six large wooden buildings surrounding a central courtyard. From the outside it gave an impression of cleanliness and order but inside the blocks conditions were very squalid. The whole of the middle of the building was taken up by a long sloping plank platform on which the convicts slept. There were no bedclothes and the entire room was littered with rags, paper, bread and miscellaneous belongings. 'It is a beastly existence, it is nihilistic, a negation of proprietary rights, privacy and comfort.' However these prisoners were relatively well off. They had no fetters and were free to walk about during the day. Escapees or those considered particularly dangerous were put 'in irons'. Here conditions were appalling with twenty men to a cell, all shackled, emaciated and half naked, and sleeping on the bare floor. They shared a common chamber pot in the corner. Chekhov looked with particular interest at the latrines and points out that this is an aspect of life to which his countrymen attach very little importance and consequently the arrangements were often extremely primitive. He mentions one prison in Kosov which had no latrine whatsoever and in which the prisoners were led out in groups to relieve themselves in the street. At Alexandrovsk, however, there was an open cesspool located in a separate out-house between the prison buildings,

PHOTO LEFT *Sakhalin convict.*

Convicts hauling logs in the Sakhalin Forest. *Photo by Chekhov.*

with the toilets lining the side of this shed. The squalor and filth of the conditions under which the convicts lived, he pointed out, must have a corrupting influence on the prisoners.

> That gregarious, animal-like existence with its gross amusements and the inevitable influence of evil on good has long been acknowledged to affect the morals of the criminal in the most corrupt fashion. It slowly forces him to lose all habits of domesticity, those very qualities which must be preserved above all by a convict who, on his release from prison, becomes a self-sufficient member of a colony, where from the first day he is obliged by law under threat of punishment, to become a good householder and a good family man.

As he watched the prisoners on the island, the questions that he continually asked himself related to the ultimate effectiveness of this method of treating criminals. He tried to understand the mental processes of the exiles in exactly the same way that he had tried to enter the world of the patients because he was convinced that only in this way could one devise strategies that worked alongside human psychology and not against it. The complete absence of any attempt at reform or rehabilitation, despite lip service to these concepts in the prison regulations, offended his therapeutic training and he pointed at example after example.

Convicts being shackled by a blacksmith. *Photo by Chekhov.*

One of the principal occupations for the prisoners was lumberjacking in the forests and hauling tree trunks for long distances over unmade roads. During this task they were harnessed to the logs by chains and in winter many of them froze to death whilst performing it. More fortunate were those who became servants to officials on the island. Some of the households hypertrophied with this cheap source of labour until they achieved ludicrous sizes. One warder boasted a seamstress, a shoemaker, a chambermaid, a footman who delivered messages, a children's nurse, a laundress, a chef and a charwoman.

Further inland, at Korsakovskoye, the medical centre had recently been closed but had housed fourteen syphilitic patients and three mental patients. One of the latter contracted syphilis. The patients of this establishment were apparently occupied making up lint dressings for the surgical department! He expostulated that hospital conditions were at least two hundred years behind civilized countries. 'If they made bonfires of lunatics by order of the prison doctors it would not surprise me.'

South of Alexandrovsk, along the coast was the grim town of Dué, set in an inlet amongst huge cliffs traversed by bands of coal, and quite devoid of vegetation. Prisoners approaching from the sea often burst into tears at the sight. The two prisons of Dué and Voyevodsk were reserved for the most violent or recidivist of prisoners, and here Chekhov saw for the first time men shackled to iron balls in conditions of dreadful overcrowding. Many of them worked in the coal mines that were alongside the prisons. The company that owned the mines, in effect five men in St Petersburg, were guaranteed an annual profit by the government of 150,000 roubles.

> What a waste of public money, and this takes no account of the fact that in order to maintain these profits, putting aside all the problems of the agricultural needs of the colony and the complete mockery of all the rules of hygiene, the treasury must maintain more than seven hundred convicts, their families, soldiers and officials in such terrifying holes like the Voyevodsk and Dué gaps.

He talked to many of the prisoners and enquired what crimes they had committed, finding them on the whole

> unexceptional looking people, with good-natured, stupid faces, expressing only curiosity and the desire to answer one as respectfully as possible. The crimes of most of them were no more intelligent or clever than their faces. They are usually sent here for five or ten years for murder committed during a fight; they escape, they are caught, again they escape, and so on, until they receive life terms as incorrigible convicts. The crimes of most of them are terribly dull, ordinary, without interest.

On the morning he left Dué

> it was raw gloomy and cold. The sea roared turbulently. I recall that on the road from the old mine to the new one we stopped for a minute near an old Caucasian who lay on the sand in a dead faint. Two of his countrymen held his hands. They kept looking round helplessly and disoncertedly. The old man was pale, his hands icy, his pulse slow. We spoke to them and went on our way without giving him any medical aid. When I mentioned to the physician who was with me that it would not have done any harm to give the old man at least some valerian drops, he said that the Voyevodsk prison had no medicines whatsoever.

Leaving the west coast, Chekhov crossed the central mountain range and descended along a tributary of the river Tym into a frozen and inhospitable area with vegetation approaching that of the tundra. He arrived one evening at a small village called Lower Armadale and was met by the local jailor who greeted him warmly but suggested that he should climb a nearby tower to sleep because at ground level 'bugs and cockroaches win all the time'.

> I climbed the tower, with a ladder that was soaked and slippery from the rain. When I descended to get my tobacco I saw the 'winning creatures' - and such things are only possible in Sakhalin. It seemed as though the walls and ceiling were covered in black crepe which stirred as if blown by the wind. From the rapid and disorderly movement of portions of this crepe you could guess at the composition of this boiling, seething mass. You could hear rustling and loud whispering as if the insects were carrying on a conversation behind your back.

The next village was Derbinskoye, which took its name from a vicious jailer who had been murdered some years previously by the prisoners beating him to death in the local bakery and throwing his body into the fermenting dough.

> That evening, until two o'clock in the morning, I sat up reading or copying data from the list of homesteads and the alphabetical list of inhabitants. The rain fell continually, rattling on the roof, and once in a while a belated prisoner or soldier passed by, slopping through the mud. It was quiet in the warehouse and in my soul, but I had scarcely put out the light and gone to bed when I heard a rustling, whispering, knocking, splashing sound and deep sighs. Raindrops fell from the ceiling and onto the latticework of the Viennese chairs and made a hollow ringing sound, and after each sound someone whispered in despair 'Oh My God, My God.' Next to the warehouse was the prison. Were the convicts coming to me through an underground passage? But then there came a gust of wind, the rain rattled even more strongly, somewhere a tree rustled and again a deep despairing sigh 'Oh My God, My God.'

> In the morning I went out on to the steps. The sky was grey and overcast, the rain continued to fall and it was muddy. The warden walked hurriedly from door to door with his keys. 'I'll give you such a ticket, you'll be scratching yourself for a week' he shouted. 'I'll show you what kind of a ticket you'll get'. These words were intended for a group a twenty prisoners who, from the few phrases

I overheard, were pleading to be sent to the hospital. They were
ragged, soaked by the rain, covered with mud and shivering. They
wanted to demonstrate in mime exactly what ailed them, but on
their pinched frozen faces it sometimes came out as false and
crooked although they were probably not lying at all. 'Oh My
God, My God', someone sighed and my nightmares seemed to be
continuing. During my entire stay in Sakhalin only in the settlers'
barracks near the mine and here in Derbinskoye, on that raining,
muddy morning did I live through moments when I felt that I saw
before me the extreme limits of man's degradation.

Chekhov had now completed his survey of the northern part of the
island and on September 10th he sailed for the south on the cruiser
Baikal in the company of an orthodox monk Iralki, (who was so
intrigued by the writer that he resolved to follow him back to Russia),
as well as a young Japanese official and the excitable wife of a naval
officer. Landing at Korsakov the principal Southern town he was met
by the district commander who turned out to be a sybarite whose main
loves were good food and French novels. Such was the effect of this
man of taste that Chekhov noted that in his district one was apt to find
not only knives, forks and wine glasses in the jailers' quarters but even
napkins: 'I found guards who were able to make tasty soup. There were
fewer fleas and cockroaches than in the North.' He walked from the
governor's house to that of the local clerk where he was dragged into
a party that was already in progress and made to drink vodka half diluted
with water and some 'very bad cognac'. He thankfully retired to bed
at two in the morning but could not sleep because a great storm was
blowing up.

The next few weeks were spent in touring the settlements of the South
but he was manifestly tiring now and 'when help was offered I graciously
accepted it.' He found the settlements and convicts here more prosperous
than those in the north although the conditions in the Korsakov prison
were bad and he made his routine tour of the latrines which he marked
down as 'smelly.' There is the usual gallery of characters that might have
strayed from his short stories such as the self-styled agricultural expert
who combined a great interest in botany with a penchant for using Latin
names. Whenever beans were served at table he said 'and this is
Phaseolus.' He called his nasty black dog Favus but his farming was a
failure. One day Chekhov entered a shop run by a retired army officer
who mistook him for an important official and began explaining that

although he had at one time been in a compromising situation he had managed to put everything right and showed him various official documents attesting to his services and character.

> Desiring to show me that he no longer owed money to anyone he began burrowing in his papers to find some receipt or other - but it was not to be found. I left the shop convinced that he was innocent and with a pound of ordinary peasant sweets. He soaked me for the sweets, charging me fifty kopeks.

At Korsakov he witnessed the arrival of a consignment of women prisoners. Since the boats carrying them had previously landed at Alexandrovsk the cream had already been skimmed and sent as servant girls to the officials or into the harems of the guards in the north. The remainder were soon distributed as follows.

> On the designated day, along the whole length to the post there can be seen travellers making their way south; these are the suitors or bridegrooms as they are called not without irony. One had put on a red bunting shirt, another wears a curious planter's hat, a third sports shining new high-heeled boots, though nobody knows where he got them from. When they arrive they are permitted to enter the women's barracks and they are left with the women. The suitors wander round the plank beds, silently and seriously eyeing the women; the latter sit with down-cast eyes. Each man makes his choice. Without any ugly grimaces, without any sneers, very seriously they act with humanity towards the old, the ugly and those with criminal features. They study the women and try to guess which of them will make good housekeepers by looking into their faces. If some younger or older woman 'reveals herself' to a man he sits down beside her and begins a serious conversation. She asks if he owns a samovar, a horse, a two-year-old heifer? Is his hut covered with planks? Only after the housekeeping examination has been completed does she venture to say 'You won't hurt me in any way, will you?'

Not all women were as fortunate as this however. Many, especially the young girls, became prostitutes. Wives were often lured into following their husbands into exile, attracted by letters describing fictitious delights that awaited them on the island. After having endured intolerable hardships and disease on the journey, their possessions were systematically stolen as soon as they landed and many were forced into brothels to support their families.

Punishments for infringements of prison discipline, particularly for acts of insubordination or violence, were savage and resorted to at the drop of a hat. The island commandant, General Kononovich, was himself opposed to corporal punishment. Nevertheless, flogging with birch rods or the more severe lashes were frequently administered. The former could be ordered for minor infringements of discipline, drunkenness or even failing to perform work tasks. Lashes were a much more inhumane affair and sometimes resulted in the death of the victim. Chekhov forced himself to witness the administration of lashes to a convict named Prokhorov who had been caught escaping and describes the whole episode in horrifying detail, including the tying down and stripping of the prisoner and his shrieks and vomiting as the strokes covered his back. After about half the ninety strokes had been administered he could stand the sight no longer and went outside for a breath of air.

> Not only do the prisoners become hardened and brutalised, but those who inflict the punishment also and so do the spectators. Educated people are no exception. At any rate, I observed that officials with university training reacted in exactly the same way as the military medical assistants or those who had completed a course in military school or an ecclesiastical seminary.

He pointed out that the savagery of the discipline was very liable to lead to further brutality from the prisoners in reprisal and that methods of punishment were being employed on Sakhalin that had long since been abandoned by civilized societies.

Despite the severe penalties for trying to escape such attempts were common on the island. Chekhov estimates that two out of every three prisoners would at some stage make a bid for freedom either in the depths of winter by walking across the ice that separates the island from mainland Siberia or in summer when the water must be crossed by raft or by stowing away on a boat and when conditions for travelling made a successful journey more likely. Many of the escapees perished from hunger or lost limbs from frostbite and most of the others were recaptured. However, the slim chance of making good their escape did not deter them from trying their luck, so powerful was their instinct for freedom. The perpetual possibility of achieving their liberty in this way was the obsession which kept a spark of vitality alight in the appalling conditions of many of the prisons. Long sentences were another incentive to escape and Chekhov pointed out that in the Korsakov region where the crops were better, the climate milder and short term prisoners predominated, the number of escape attempts were strikingly fewer than in the northern part of the island.

In the last chapter of the book *The Island of Sakhalin* in which he describes his journey Chekhov the doctor turned his attention to the diseases and mortality statistics. He had examined the reports of illnesses of the convict population submitted for the previous year and looked through the church records for the causes of death over a ten year period. He was well aware of the shortcomings of most of these reports and presented his data with a lively sense of its limitations.

> Because of the inadequacy of both these sources everything the reader finds below concerning sickness and mortality is not a true picture but merely a meagre sketch.

The care with which he presented these facts and particularly his reluctance to indulge in random speculation where evidence was not available suggests that, if he had not been otherwise engaged, he might well have made outstanding contributions in the field of epidemiology and public health.

He noted the infrequency of the recognised acute infections with which he was familiar in European Russia. Even smallpox, which had once annihilated whole tribes in Japan and Kamchatka was comparatively uncommon. He remarked, rather curiously, that

> pockmarked faces are frequently seen among the Gilyaks (the aboriginal inhabitants of Northern Sakhalin) but this was due to chickenpox (varicella) which in all probability is not infectious among foreigners.

This was certainly *not* chickenpox (which does not leave scars) but may have been a relatively benign strain of smallpox. Typhus and typhoid were also relatively uncommon but Chekhov observed that there was a common 'inexactly definable feverish illness' which occurred especially during the winter season and sometimes manifested a rosealar rash. it lasted from five to seven days and as many of the patients did not report sick but lay on their stoves in their houses it was probably much more prevalent than the recorded numbers suggested. A common respiratory illness with a high death-rate (30%) was called 'croupous pneumonia' and seemed to have two peaks of incidence - one in the middle of winter and another in May or June. The physician of the local infirmary to whom Chekhov talked attributed this disease to the hauling of heavy logs along snow-covered roads. Dysentery and cholera were not conspicuous nor were there any reports of malaria. Tuberculosis, however, was a frequent cause of death, the highest mortality being in the age group 25-35. Most of those affected were convicts and he attributed the prevalence to deprivations, overcrowding and underfeeding. Syphilis, particularly in its secondary and tertiary stage was also common and many of these chronically disabled patients were extremely pathetic and hardly ever had a medical inspection.

Scurvy, the nature of which was still obscure, occurred frequently although it had been even more ubiquitous ten years previously. It was commonly found in shiploads of prisoners at the end of their long journey. On May 2nd, 1890, for instance, the St Petersburg landed 500 prisoners, 100 of whom were suffering from scurvy. Knowing now the cause to be a deficiency of Vitamin C, it is interesting to read that 'some of the old writers praised wild garlick as a marvellous preventive of scurvy.' In view of the conditions under which the convicts lived and worked it is not surprising that injuries, acts of violence, suicide and murder bulked high in the statistics.

The only substantial infirmary on the island was at Alexandrovsk. This had 180 beds and comprised several buildings made of wooden logs. He passed a well-kept and gleaming dispensary, resplendent with a bust of Botkin and boxes full of medicinal bark and roots. The wards, however, were filthy and patients neglected. A convict who had cut his throat had been left with an open undressed wound from which air was escaping. Cheek by jowl with this open wound was a Chinese with gangrene. Next to him on the left, a case of erysipelas, a highly infectious disease, and in the corner another with the same. The dressings that he saw looked exactly as if they had been walked on. In the consulting room for ambulant patients the doctor sat enclosed in a wooden lattice

> like a banker's office, so that during the examination the patient
> never comes close to the doctor, who in the majority of cases
> examines him from a distance, whilst a soldier with a revolver
> stands at the door. A young boy is brought in with an abscess on
> his neck. It needs lancing. I ask for a scalpel. The medical assistant

and two men jump up from their seats and run off; they return in a little while and hand me a scalpel. The instrument is blunt, but they tell me that is impossible because the blacksmith sharpened it recently. Again the assistant and men jump up and after two or three minutes they bring me another scalpel. I begin to make an incision and this scalpel also proves to be blunt. I ask for carbolic acid; they bring it to me but they take their time. It is obvious that carbolic acid is seldom used. There is no basin, no cotton balls, no probes, no good scissors and not even enough water.

Even Chekhov's usual patience was at an end.

After three months exhausting work on the island he decided to come home by sea and on October 13th sailed on the liner *St Petersburg*. He had been given a warm send-off by a deputation of officials who organised a farewell dinner, and by a less organised but obviously affectionately disposed group of convicts who insisted on carrying him in their cart from the dinner to the embarkation point. The ship called at Vladivostock where he was appalled at the filth and poverty, Hong Kong where he was much impressed by the sight of the bay and had words of praise for the English colonial administration, and lastly Ceylon,

the site of Paradise. Here I covered some seventy miles by rail and had my fill of palm groves and bronze-skinned women. When I have children I'll say to them, not without pride; 'You fellows, in my time I made love to a dark-eyed Hindu maiden - where? - in a coconut grove on a starlit night.'[10]

After this well earned *dolce far niente* the long crawl through the Red Sea and back to Odessa was hot and boring. Conditions on board the ship must have suggested to him the subject of his short story *Gussev* in which he describes the death and burial of two convicts on board a troop ship in the middle-east.

Back in Moscow, he set to work putting his mountains of notes and statistics together in a continuous account. He felt a sense of elation at having accomplished so much.

I am up to my chin in satisfaction and am so enchanted that I wish

---

[10] A. Chekhov. Letter to A.S. Suvorin. 9 December 1890.

for nothing more and would not feel wronged if I were struck down
by paralysis or carried off to the next world by dysentery.[11]

But the writing of *The Island of Sakhalin* did not come easily to him.
He found the endless references and statistics tedious - and his groaning
over being 'forced for the sake of a single mangy line or other to
rummage among papers for a full hour'[12] must strike a familiar note to
anyone acquainted with writing scientific papers. It took him over three
years to complete the book which was serialised in part by the Journal
Russian Thought and published in full in 1894, although one of the
chapters had been separately published in 1891 to help the famine
victims. Reading it today, the exemplariness of the writing, the systematic
way in which he presents the statistics with a realistic view of their
limitations and above all the concise recommendations for action put
forward with a hard-headed understanding of the practical and financial
implications are quite astonishing in a writer whose fame had been
established in the field of imaginative fiction. Chekhov consulted his
friend Rossolimo who was then a lecturer at the Moscow Medical
School, and later became a professor, about the possibility of submitting
it for an MD thesis. Rossolimo had been anxious for some time to invite
him to give a course of lectures to the students to make them understand
what it felt like to be ill, to encourage them to identify with patients of
all descriptions. This imaginative project would have required Chekhov
to have a post-graduate qualification, so Rossolimo enquired of the Dean
of the Medical School about both the MD thesis and the course of
lectures, but the Dean simply smiled ironically and walked away without
speaking.

The work was not wasted however, for after its publication *The Island
of Sakhalin* drew attention to the plight of the convicts and a government
commission was sent out to the island in 1896 to investigate and make
recommendations. Chekhov was haunted by the thought of the children
he had met on the island and organised the dispatch of thousands of books
to the Sakhalin schools. It was an episode that he could rightly feel proud
of and although he made strangely little use of themes from this journey
in his subsequent fiction and plays, he recognised that he had now paid
his 'debt to medicine' and could turn for a time to other pastures. He
wrote to Suvorin

---

[11] A. Chekhov. Letter to I.N. Leontyev-Shcheglov. 10 December 1890.
[12] A. Chekhov. Letter to A.S. Suvorin. 27 May 1891.

I have rendered just tribute to learning and to that which the old writers used to call pedantry. And I rejoice because the rough garb of the convict will also be hanging in my wardrobe. Let it hang there.[13]

[13] A. Chekhov. Letter to A.S. Suvorin. 2 January 1894.

CHAPTER V

Tolstoy versus Science

In 1890 Tolstoy published his short story *The Kreutzer Sonata*. The Russian censor immediately banned it for outraging public decency. Such was the authority and following of the author however, that secret copies were soon put into circulation. It was one of these clandestine copies that Chekhov read. He was so impressed by it that, when his friend and literary editor Alexei Pleshcheyev expressed his hostility to it, he protested;

> Do you really mean that you do not like *The Kreutzer Sonata*? I won't say it is a work of genius. I cannot judge these things. But in my opinion, of all the mass of writing that is being produced here and abroad you will hardly find anything to touch it in importance of conception and beauty of execution.[1]

He had reservations about the factual content of the story, particularly on sexual and medical matters but

> ....these faults are easily dispersed as feathers before the wind. The greatness of the piece is such that they pass unnoticed.

Chekhov's attitude towards *The Kreutzer Sonata* however was soon to change. By December of 1890, on his return from Sakhalin, he was writing to Suvorin,

> Before my journey *The Kreutzer Sonata* seemed a major event but

---

PHOTO LEFT
Chekhov and Tolstoy.

[1] A. Chekhov. Letter to A.M. Pleshcheyev. 15 February 1890.

now I find it absurd and confused. Either the journey has matured me or I have gone quite mad, the devil alone knows which.[2]

Whilst he was away Tolstoy had written an 'Afterword' to his story making its message even more explicit. Chekhov read it with growing distaste and indignation.

> Diogenes spat on people's beards knowing that he would not be called to account. Tolstoy calls doctors scoundrels and flaunts his ignorance of important matters because he is a second Diogenes whom no one will report to the police or denounce to the newspapers. So to hell with the philosophy of the great men of the world.

What was the nature of this short story that was causing such consternation to the Russian censor and to Chekhov?

Whatever the reactions of the reader to its moral stance no one would dispute that it is wonderfully written. Set in a railway carriage the story recounts the conversation between an 'advanced' young lady, her lawyer friend, an elderly tradesman and the story's writer. The talk revolves around the status and rights of women, a subject on which the tradesman has stern and illiberal views. 'Don't trust your horse in the field or your wife in the house', is the core of his philosophy. When he leaves the compartment all the others roundly condemn him and extol the virtues of love in marriage, all, that is, with the exception of a diffident grey-haired man in the corner who now joins in the conversation. What is this love that is supposed to sanctify marriage? How long does it last? Is it not frequently, if we are honest, nothing but lust, and marriages as they exist in reality, either reduced to deception or coercion, generators of hatred rather than love?

To the astonishment of his fellow passengers he then reveals that he is the notorious criminal Pozdnyshev who had been condemned for the brutal murder of his wife in a fit of jealousy and who had been released after a period of imprisonment. The compartment soon empties in alarm with the exception of Pozdnyshev and the storyteller and, as night comes on, the latter persuades the murderer to tell him the history of his life; it is this narration that takes up most of the remaining part of the story.

---

[2] A. Chekhov. Letter to A.S. Suvorin. 17 December 1890.

In the account that he gives of the breakdown of his marriage Tolstoy, through Pozdnyshev, takes the lid off the institution as he sees it and reveals a state of affairs that he regards as altogether shocking and morally unacceptable. Many marriages are nothing more than licensed debauchery. The woman is taught to regard herself as an object of sexual satisfaction for her husband even at times when she gets no pleasure from it herself or when she cannot conceive, in pregnancy or suckling. Worse, doctors are instructing women how to copulate and avoid having children and are only too ready to encourage men in the belief that they must have sex and that restraint is bad for them. So the doctors connive in double standards and insist on government inspection of brothels to make sure that syphilis is not spread.

Anticipating some arguments now being advanced about the spread of AIDS he denounces the doctors.

> Why, who are these doctors? They call themselves priests of science and yet deprave the youth by maintaining that this is necessary for their health. Yet if a hundredth part of the efforts devoted to the cure of syphilis were applied to the eradication of debauchery there would long ago not have been a trace of syphilis left.

The result of this whole attitude is the degradation of a woman into a plaything. A whole industry has grown up about adorning her person. With its aid she is virtually sold into bondage and maintained as a sort of unpaid prostitute. Is it surprising then that she uses the only levers of power that are left in her hands, her sexual attractions, and that many marriages degenerate, as Pozdnyshev's had done, into a living hell in which endless vituperation is punctuated by brief loveless sexual relations, until the cycle is broken by the prospect of another romantic attachment? So called education is often no more than a reinforcement of men's views of the role of women in society.

Doctors are the particular object of censure.

> I would willingly give them half my income, and all who realise what they are doing would freely give them half their possessions, if only they would not interfere with our family lives and would never come near us

Pozdnyshev roundly declares.

> I have not collected evidence but I know dozens of cases (there are
> any number of them) where they have killed a child in the mother's
> womb asserting that she could not give it birth, although the
> mother went on to have childbirth quite safely later on. No one
> calls these murders any more than the killings of the Inquisition
> were called murder, because it is claimed that they are done for the
> good of mankind.

Not only are the doctors abortionists but they are amoral in their
attitude to life.

> Today one can no longer say 'You're not living rightly. Live
> better'. One cannot say that to oneself or to anyone else. If you
> live a bad life it is due to the abnormal functioning of one's nerves
> etc. So you must go to them and they will prescribe eight penn'orth
> of medicine from the chemist which you must take.

And then, when children come there is no relief from the impositions
of the doctors who take advantage of the anxieties of mothers over the
illnesses of their children to encourage visits to some particular authority
or specialist who claims fraudulently to have saved the lives of thousands
of children with his medicines.

> Catherine Semenovna lost two children because Ivan Zaharych
> was not called in time, but Ivan Zaharych saved Mary Ivanovna's
> eldest girl, and the Petrovs moved in time to various hotels at the
> doctor's advice and the children survived, but if they had not been
> segregated the children would have died.

So, fear and superstition are encouraged in the name of science and
all this distorts men and women's natural lives, lives which the peasants
have lived for centuries with their simple virtues and humility. It is this
unnatural distortion that encourages diseases such as hysteria, with
which Charcot's clinics in Paris are full, and which drives marital
relations to the point of breakdown. It was this that drove Pozdnyshev's
marriage along its stormy course until the inevitable infidelity, hatred
and jealousy led to the murder of his wife. It is a situation made all the
worse because it is propagated in the name of enlightenment and made
respectable by professional practitioners.

Such was Tolstoy's indictment of the attitude of society towards marriage in *The Kreutzer Sonata*. A.N. Wilson in his recent biography warns against any direct indentification of the opinions that Tolstoy puts into the mouth of Pozdnyshev, the murderer, with those of the author,[3] and it is of course a commonplace of the novelist's art that the imagination will use and transform the realities of ordinary life in the creation of fictional characters. The genre embarked on is, as Wilson remarks, nearer to that of Dostoyevsky or Maupassant than to Tolstoy's usual realistic mode. His contemporaries, including Chekhov, however saw that, even if the opinions were sharpened or made absurd at times, perhaps with the intention of shocking, they were very close to Tolstoy's own views, and they have to be seen in the context of the much wider critique of society to be found in his later works. For Tolstoy, the older institutions had lost what authority they once had. The government, the law and the institutionalised church were hopelessly corrupt and self-seeking. He had come to believe that the only forces in life that are worth striving for are the simple moral virtues; love, compassion, forgiveness. Society as it exists does not recognise them. Even science, he now claims is destroying the very basis on which they were once able to thrive.

He found these virtues exemplified in the lives of the peasants and regarded civilization, culture, sophistication of any kind, as deeply destructive of such natural ideals. We see the influence here of the ideas of Rousseau whose works had been thoroughly absorbed by Tolstoy in his youth and remained a model for his moral philosophy.

In *What Then Must We Do* which Tolstoy published in 1886,[4] and which as we shall see, Chekhov had obviously read, he gives a moving and vivid description of the plight of the Moscow poor, whom he had encountered for the first time on going to live in the city. With an indignation that reminds one of Dickens in his days as a reporter, he indicts a society that can tolerate gross inequalities of wealth, starvation and filth rubbing shoulders with ostentatious luxury. He regards the whole of civilization as designed to perpetuate this injustice, and includes in his indictment science and the medical profession. The sociological theories of August Comte which used the analogy of society as a biological organism to justify inequalities as inevitable to specialization of function, or the theories of Darwin and Malthus which expounded the struggle and survival of the fittest, were being used to preserve the status quo. Science

---

[3] A.N. Wilson. *Tolstoy*. Hamish Hamilton. 1988. pp. 373-391
[4] Leo Tolstoy. *What Then Must We Do?* Translated by Aylmer Maude. Oxford University Press. 1925.

in its practical applications adapted itself to the divided state of society and brought its benefits, trains, telegraph, electricity, expensive forms of health care to the rich, leaving the poor untouched.

> The doctor ...... needs an endless number of expensive appliances, instruments, medicaments, and hygienically arranged rooms, food and water-closets to enable him to act scientifically; ..... He has studied in the capitals under celebrities who only take patients who can be treated in hospital, or who while being treated can purchase the apparatus needed for the treatment, and can even travel immediately from the north to the south, or to such and such watering-places. Their science is of such a kind that every zemstvo doctor complains of not having the means to treat the labourers; that they are so poor that it is impossible to place the patients in hygienic conditions; that there are no hospitals, that he cannot manage all the work and that he needs more assistants, doctors and trained helpers. What does this mean? It means that the chief calamity of the people, causing illness to arise and spread and remain untreated, is the insufficiency of their means of livelihood.

Chekhov could clearly say 'Amen' to this and indeed it is a distinct pre-echo of those who today point to the 'health divide' between the rich and poor as one of the medical challenges of our time. Tolstoy argued that more attention should be paid to lifestyle as a cause of disease.

> The sphere of medicine, unlike that of engineering, lies as yet untouched. All the questions of how best to divide the worktime, how best to nourish oneself, on what and in what form, when and how it is best to clothe oneself, to cover one's feet, to resist dampness and cold, how best to wash and feed the children, swaddle them, and so forth, in the actual circumstances in which the working people live - all these questions have not yet been asked.

He attributes many of the ills of the upper classes to the lack of exercise, and the complex remedies for this state of affairs as merely tinkering with the effects instead of tackling the cause.

> The profound complexities of medicine and hygiene for people of our class are such as a mechanic might devise in order, when he has

heated a boiler and screwed down all the valves, to prevent the boiler bursting. And when I clearly understood all this, it seemed to me ludicrous. By a long series of doubts, searchings and reflection, I have reached the extraordinary truth that man has eyes in order to see with them, legs in order to walk with them, and hands and a back to work with, and that if he does not use them for their natural purpose it will be the worse for him.

Tolstoy instinctively rejected any dependence on experts, technicians, professionals, whom he suspected of being in a conspiracy to increase the power of rich over the poor. Anything that smacked of what we would call 'high tech' medicine was to be distrusted. In a final chapter he turns to the situation of women, and as in *The Kreutzer Sonata,* sees in the emergence of contraception, a threat to the moral welfare of women's lives.

Chekhov greatly admired Tolstoy as a writer throughout his life. In the Pantheon of Russian arts he placed Tolstoy first, with Tchaikovsky second. Indeed, for a time in the mid eighties there are unmistakable influences of Tolstoy's ideas on his writings. Looking back at this period he wrote to Suvorin in 1894,

> Tolstoy's philosophy moved me deeply and possessed me for six or seven years. It was not so much his basic postulates that had an effect on me - I had been familiar with them before - it was his way of expressing himself, his common sense, and probably a sort of hypnotism as well.[5]

Tolstoy for his part early recognised Chekhov's genius and helped him to get a publisher for his collected works. He was particularly fond of the story *The Darling* and would read it aloud to the family.

In time they became firm friends and when news of one of Tolstoy's illnesses reached him Chekhov wrote:

> I fear Tolstoy's death. It would leave an empty space in my life. I have loved no man as much as him. I am not a believer but of all beliefs I consider his to be the closest to my thoughts and the most suitable for me. When literature has a Tolstoy it is easy and

---

[5] A. Chekhov. Letter to A.S. Suvorin. 27 March 1894.

gratifying to be a writer. Even when you are not accomplishing anything you don't feel too bad because Tolstoy accomplishes enough for everyone.[6]

In their attitude to moral questions, to the nature and importance of science and the virtues of civilisation and culture however the two writers came to differ fundamentally.

> Maybe its because I've given up smoking, but Tolstoy's philosophy has ceased to move me; deep down I'm hostile to it which of course is unfair. I have peasant blood flowing in my veins, and I'm not the one to be impressed by peasant virtues. I acquired my belief in progress while still a child. I couldn't help believing in it because the difference between the period when they flogged me and the period when they stopped flogging me was enormous. I've always loved intelligent people, heightened sensibilities, courtesy and wit, and paid as little attention to whether people pick their corns or have suffocatingly smelly footcloths as to whether young ladies walk around in the morning with curlpapers on..... Prudence and justice tell me there is more love for mankind in electricity and steam than in chastity and abstention from meat. War is an evil and the court system is an evil, but it doesn't follow that I should wear bast shoes and sleep on a stove alongside the hired hand and his wife, and so on and so forth. But that's not the issue; its not a matter of the pros and cons. The point is that one way or another Tolstoy has departed from my life. He's no longer in my heart and he's left me saying 'Behold, I leave your house empty'. He dwells in me no longer. I'm tired of listening to disquisitions and reading phonies like Max Nordau.

Nordau, a Hungarian doctor, had made his name by publishing a book *Entartung,* Degeneracy, in which he forecast the decline of Western man on biological grounds but backed up by a pseudo-philosophical apparatus designed to prove that Western culture was hopelessly decadent, anticipating Spengler's *Decline of the West* fifty years later. Chekhov, an empiricist to the marrow, had no time for these wide-sweeping theses and saw in his contemporaries a hunger for something more substantial.

---

[6] A. Chekhov. Letter to M. Menshikov. 28 January 1900.

It's as though everyone has been in love and got over it, and was looking around for new interests. It looks very likely that Russians will once again become absorbed in the natural sciences and that materialism will come back in style. The natural sciences are at present working miracles, and they can advance on the populace like Mamai and subdue it by their sheer mass and grandeur. But of course, all this lies in the hand of God. And if you start philosophising it'll only make you dizzy.[7]

Chekhov's optimism about general social progress and about the part that science would play in bringing this about has to be seen in the context of his times, heady times for the medical faculty. The last half of the nineteenth century had witnessed a complete transformation in the outlook for many diseases. Joseph Lister, working in Glasgow, and on the basis of Pasteur's work in Paris, inaugurated antisepsis in surgery, publishing his work in the Lancet in 1867. This, together with anaesthesia which had been brought into general use by James Simpson of Edinburgh in the previous decade, opened the way for a whole generation of surgeons, many of them German, who explored every area of the body. The first removal of a gall-bladder was performed in 1878, the first appendicectomy in 1886. Robert Koch's discoveries of the bacterial origin of tuberculosis in 1882 and of the cholera vibrio in 1883 (whilst Chekhov was at Moscow Medical School) were throwing light on the causes of infectious disease and providing an impetus for public health measures that were reducing the high level of infant mortality. Looking back on these years, William Osler, the doyen of Western physicians, wrote in January 1901

> The Promethean gift of the nineteenth century to man was the decrease of physical suffering in man, woman and child when stricken by disease and accident. To us, whose work is with the sick and suffering the great boon of this wonderful century, with which no other can be compared, is the fact that the leaves of the tree of science have been for the healing of the nations.[8]

If conditions in the Russian countryside were still primitive, if superstition rather than rational medicine was still clung to, there was

---

[7] A. Chekhov. Letter to A.S. Suvorin. 27 March 1894.

[8] W. Osler. *Aequanimitas with other addresses*. Lewis. London. 1939. p. 262

now a light at the end of the tunnel. Cleanliness was replacing godliness as a rule of life for many of the young doctors, who received the undoubted achievements of science as a rallying cry to action. During the cholera epidemic of 1892 Chekhov wrote to Suvorin

> In the good old days when people fell ill and died by the thousand no one would have dreamed of the astounding victories taking place before our eyes. It's a shame that you are not a doctor and cannot share my pleasure, that is, deeply realise and appreciate everything that is happening.[9]

The obverse side of the coin of scientific progress, the price that has to be paid, which is evident to us at the end of the twentieth century, was not apparent a hundred years ago, when threats such as overpopulation, pollution of the environment and sophisticated weapons technology had not yet arrived. Nor was it evident, as we find it today, that the increase in knowledge and power, far from providing answers to man's moral problems, simply increases the number and complexity of problems without itself providing the solutions. Tolstoy's hostility to science was no doubt in part due to culpable ignorance. Chekhov commented that he was unwilling to pardon the author of *The Kreutzer Sonata* for

> the audacity with which he treats topics which he doesn't understand and doesn't wish to understand. So, for example, his opinions about syphilis, foundling homes, women's revulsion for sexual intercourse and so on are not merely disputable but they unmask an ignorant man who hasn't taken the trouble in the course of his long life to read two or three books written by specialists.[10]

A.N. Wilson entitles this aspect of Tolstoy's pontificating 'bronchitis is a metal' after a remark that the author made to Turgenyev who said he thought he had an attack of bronchitis. But underlying Tolstoy's deep scepticism about science and technology and his contempt for any naive faith in man's reasoning powers was a perception of an altogether more interesting kind than 'bronchitis is a metal'. It was based on Tolstoy's awareness of the complexities of the patterns of causation, the infinite

---

[9] A. Chekhov. Letter to A.S. Suvorin. 16 August 1892.
[10] A. Chekhov. Letter to A. Pleshcheyev. 15 February 1890.

variety of human responses that refused to be categorised, and he combined this insight with a deep distrust for experts and technicians in the field of human affairs who might well be simply increasing their power and influence over others whilst invading areas in which they had no competence.

Isaiah Berlin in his essay on Tolstoy, *The Hedgehog and the Fox* [11], contrasts those writers whose gift it is to see life in all its teeming complexity, who rejoice in the idiosyncracy of the human condition, with those other writers who pursue some great synoptic vision underlying the complexities of experience, whether such a vision takes the form of a religious unity, a historical destiny or a biological continuum. He takes his title from a fragment by Archilocus: 'The fox knows many things but the hedgehog knows one big thing.' Berlin's thesis is that Tolstoy was by nature a fox. This is, *par excellence*, the gift of the great realist, the author of *War and Peace* and *Anna Karenina*, who had used his unrivalled capacity to empathise with and to characterise a great range of men and women, young and old, even the dogs. It was this aspect of his genius that attracted and inspired Chekhov, who was to become, perhaps, one of the greatest 'foxes' in literature. But, to the indignation of Tolstoy, this disciple 'fox' was also a doctor, a scientist, a categoriser. 'Medicine stands in his way' he growled to Gorki. 'He would have been a much finer writer if he hadn't been a doctor.' [12]

But, if Tolstoy, according to Berlin, was a natural 'fox' he also felt the necessity to behave like a hedgehog. He needed some overall vision to save appearances, to redeem the world from a meaningless and frightening pluralism, and he found this in a non-dogmatic ethical Christianity derived from the Sermon on the Mount. What he thought he detected in Chekhov, attributing this to his medical training, was an absence of any moral attitude, an indifference to the way people behave. 'Chekhov was with us, and I liked him very much' he wrote to his son Leo in 1895. 'He is very talented and must have a good heart, but so far has given no evidence of possessing a definite point of view.' [13]

For Chekhov it was no part of a writer's task to sit as a judge on his characters, far less to provide answers to life's problems in the direct way that Tolstoy was attempting to do. From his experience of scientific method he drew the moral that it was only through the discipline of

---

[11] Isaiah Berlin. *The Hedgehog and the Fox, in Russian Thinkers*. The Hogarth Press Ltd. 1978.
[12] M. Gorki. *A. Chekhov*. Moscow. 1937. p.108.
[13] E.J. Simmons. *Chekhov: a biography*. Little, Brown and Co. 1962. p. 568.

acknowledging our fundamental ignorance of life and human beings that understanding will eventually be achieved.

> You are right to demand that an author take conscious stock of what he is doing, but you are confusing two concepts: answering the questions and formulating them properly

he wrote to Suvorin.

> Only the latter is required of an author. There's not a single question answered in *Anna Karenina* or *Eugene Onegin*, but they are still fully satisfying works because the questions they raise are all formulated correctly. It is up to each member of the jury to answer them according to his own preference.[14]

Commenting on a criticism of one of his stories *The Steppe* he made a parallel distinction between the 'method' of the critic and his 'views'.

> It's not important that he has definite opinions, convictions, a world view. Anyone has those at a given time. The important thing is that he has a method. For the analyst, whether he is scientist or critic, the method constitutes half the talent.[15]

This emphasis on method must have come directly from his scientific training. It can be found clearly stated in the writings of the great neuropsychiatrist Pavlov, with whose writings Chekhov would have been well acquainted.

> Method is the most basic consideration. The seriousness of research depends on the method used, on the means of action. The whole edifice relies on a valid method. With such a method, even a man with limited abilities can do much, whereas without this a genius will work in vain.[16]

Another seminal writer was Claude Bernard the French physiologist

---

14 A. Chekhov. Letter to A.S. Suvorin. 27 October 1888.
15 A. Chekhov. Letter to A. Pleshcheyev. 6 March 1888.
16 E.B. Meve. *op. cit.* Chapter 1.

whose *Introduction to Experimental Medicine* was in Chekhov's library. When Shcheglov-Leontyev criticised him for ending a story with 'You can't understand anything in this world', saying that an artist who is also a psychologist 'must be able to understand people, or why is he a psychologist?' Chekhov replied

> I don't agree with him. It's about time that writers, especially those with literary aspirations, admitted that in this world you can't be certain of anything. Socrates admitted it once upon a time. The crowd thinks and knows it understands everything; the stupider it is the broader it imagines its outlook. But, if a writer whom people respect takes it upon himself to declare he understands nothing of what he sees, that alone will constitute a major gain in the realm of thought, and a big step forward.[17]

This is not to suggest of course that Chekhov did not have firm moral convictions of his own, even if he did not have an imposing world view. He agreed at times that his stories did imply attitudes even if they did not state them explicitly.

> You once told me

he wrote to Pleshcheyev about his story *The Party*,

> that my stories lack an element of protest, that they have neither sympathies nor antipathies. But doesn't the story protest against lying from start to finish? Isn't that an ideology? It isn't? Well I guess that means that either I don't know how to bite or I am a flea.[18]

The important thing for him was, not to be morally neutral or indifferent, which would involve culpable lack of concern for the many evils with which life abounds, but to realise that by imposing moral values on the reader, the writer loses his claim to objectivity, to be able to describe life as it really is, just as a doctor who moralizes to his patients, as the opinionated Dr Lvov does in Ivanov, loses credibility with the

---

[17] A. Chekhov. Letter to A.S. Suvorin. 30 May 1888.
[18] A. Chekhov. Letter to A.N. Pleshcheyev. 9 October 1888.

person he is trying to help. The creative writer must renounce everyday subjectivity and, as Chekhov said to Ivan Bunin 'be ice-cold before sitting down to write'[19] if he wants to move his reader.

Chekhov's reaction to Tolstoy's ideas can be traced in many of his stories. In the years between his graduation and the journey to Sakhalin there are a number of the stories that are Tolstoyan in the sense that they directly advocate virtues rated highly by Tolstoy such as non-violence (*The Encounter*) or the transforming power of love (*The Beggar*) and, exceptionally, in 1894 this philosophy returns in *The Head Gardener's Story*. With his emancipation from Tolstoy's spell in the nineties, however, there emerged a group of stories in which Tolstoyism is subjected to a critique by example. In *The Duel* of 1891, Tolstoy's influence is claimed for one of the characters. This is followed by *The Artist's Story* (1895) in which Tolstoy's arguments on work are urged at length, and finally by *My Life* (1896) in which his philosophy is put to the test. Each of the stories contains a spokesman, as it were, for the scientific view, but, in observance of his own rules, Chekhov tries to preserve impartiality and avoid biasing the reader's sympathy in favour of his own opinions by giving each of these spokesmen major flaws of character. Conversely, the advocates of Tolstoy's philosophy in two of the stories are given the psychological advantage of being first person narrators.

The Duel is a long and complex story set in the Crimea. The two chief protagonists, Laevsky and Von Koren, whose incompatibility leads to a furious argument, one of the many verbal encounters in the Chekhov canon, and a subsequent demand for satisfaction, justify their attitudes to life by appealing to Tolstoy and science respectively. Laevsky has many of the features of that favourite character in Russian literature, christened if not invented by Turgenyev, the superfluous man. These ineffectuals, racked by middle-age crises, washed up and depressed, had an appeal for Chekhov and are often treated engagingly if not exactly with sympathy. One thinks of Ivanov, Vanya and Gayev in the plays. Laevsky is distinctly *not* likeable however, and is addicted to lying which is never a trivial matter with his author. With a certain impudence he claims Tolstoy for his model in life.

> I must find an explanation, an excuse for my futile life in somebody's theories, in literary types - say in the fact that we the gentry are

---

[19] I.A. Bunin. *O Chekhove: Nezakouchennaya rakopis*. New York. 1953.

going to the bad, and so on. Last night, for instance, I kept consoling myself with the thought of Tolstoy. He's so right about things. So fiendishly right. And it made me feel better. He's really a great writer, old man, say what you like.

Laevsky once belonged to the Arts Faculty at St Petersburg University and he still subscribes to two literary reviews. Falling in love with a married woman he has escaped to the Caucasus but now he has fallen out of love with her and taken to drink. His way of life would have been deeply repugnant to Tolstoy and his appeal to Tolstoy's philosophy is obviously bogus, a mere excuse or rationalization, but an example perhaps of how such a world view can be made to justify indifference or nihilism.

If Laevsky is unattractive, however, his opponent from the Science Faculty, Von Koren, is no better. He is everything that Laevsky is not; hard working, meticulous, intolerant, impatient and egotistical. A zoologist by profession, he is engaged in researching the fauna of the Black Sea, although Laevsky says that he has it on good authority that the area is very poor in animal life owing to the accumulation of hydrogen sulphide and reports a rumour that the biologist only works here in isolation because he has fallen out with his academic colleagues. Von Koren's scientific ideas are as intolerant as his personality. He appeals to Darwin's concept of the survival of the fittest to justify elimination of the sick and degenerate, including such 'specimens' as Laevsky. True love, as he explains to his friend the deacon, in the course of a lengthy apologia for his philosophy of life, consists in the victory of the strong over the weak. It is inevitable that these two pathological and slightly absurd representatives of the two cultures will clash and their subsequent duel has a symbolic as well as literal inevitability. Appropriately, neither contestant is seriously hurt and, in a somewhat unconvincing final chapter they both decide to mend their ways and are reconciled, the one false note in an otherwise magnificently told tale. It is however more interesting as a clash of personalities than because of any views expressed. The ideas move into focus in *The Artist's Story*.

The exponent of Tolstoyism here is the artist of the title, a landscape painter, and as he engagingly admits, 'one of nature's idlers'. It was whilst he was staying on the estate of a landowner friend one summer that he came across the house of the Volchaninov family, a widowed mother and her two daughters Lydia and Zhenya. Lydia, the elder, spends all her time and energy trying to help the peasants, treating their illnesses (although she has apparently no medical qualifications), teaching in the village school and sitting on the district council. She is a severe and socially aware young woman and has no sympathy whatsoever for this dissolute young man who has apparently fallen for her sister and has the temerity to paint pictures which do not depict the hardship of the peasants.

One afternoon they fall to discussing the need, as Lydia sees it, for a local medical clinic in the village. The painter says that he sees no need for such a clinic. Lydia, irritated by this ill-informed comment, explains that if a clinic had existed they would have avoided the death in childbirth that she had just witnessed there. The painter then goes into a long explanation of how clinics, schools, libraries only serve to enslave the peasants, not relieve their lot.

> You go to their aid with hospitals and schools, but that's not freeing them from their shackles, oh dear me no. It's only a worse form of slavery, because by bringing these new fads into their lives you increase their needs, quite apart from their having to pay the council for these poultices and books and so having to work even harder.

'I shan't argue with you' said Lydia, lowering her newspaper. 'I've heard all that before. I'll just say this. We can't all sit down twiddling our thumbs. It's true we're not saving mankind, and we may be getting a lot of things wrong, but we're doing what we can and we're on the right lines. Serving one's fellow men, a civilised person can't do anything finer or nobler than that.'

The artist insists however, that what is needed is

> to free them from heavy manual work. Lighten their load. Give them a breathing space so they don't spend all their lives at the stove and washtub, or in the fields, but also have time to think about their souls, about God, and to develop the life of the spirit. When Lydia sardonically asks how one is to free them from work he answers that 'if all we townsfolk and country people, every man jack of us, agreed to share the work done by mankind as a whole to satisfy physical needs, we might not have to do more than two or three hours work each day. If we didn't take medicine and had no doctors, chemists, tobacco factories or distilleries, what a lot of

leisure that would give us in the end, and we'd all join in devoting our leisure to science and the arts.'

This is drawn, with only minor alterations, directly from chapter 38 of Tolstoy's *What Then Must We Do* and clearly identifies the narrator as a full subscriber to Tolstoy's philosophy of the necessity for all to do manual labour. There is rich irony in it being propounded by 'one of nature's idlers'. Lydia, seeing that her sister is falling for this wastrel, persuades her mother to take Zhenya for a prolonged visit to an aunt in a distant province. The idyll is over.

Strangely, Ronald Hingley, in his introduction to the story [20], sees Chekhov's sympathies as being entirely with the narrator and against the priggish Lydia and thinks there may be an implied moral that 'private life is more important than public postures.' He also refers in an appendix to an argument that Chekhov is said to have had with the daughter of the publisher V.M. Lavrov on the position of the Russian peasant. According to a witness Chekhov 'embodied his own views on this matter in the ardent speech of the landscape painter in *The Artist's Story*.' This seems very unlikely, unless we are to regard him as endorsing the views that medicine and doctors can be dispensed with and that medical clinics are not needed by the peasants at the very time he was working as a doctor at Melikhova, with his sister Marya as his unpaid and unqualified assistant. She must have been left on many occasions with the same responsibilities as Lydia. One must also take into account that the whole story is seen through the eyes of the artist, including the character of Lydia, and that he was hardly likely to have painted a sympathetic portrait of someone who had stolen his girl friend.

The same problem is presented by any attempt to come to terms with the narrator of the third of these stories, *My Life*, although his self-disparagement makes one want to believe him and he is certainly not idle. Misail is twentyfour, the son of an architect in a small provincial town. Unsuccessful in holding down the boring clerical jobs that he is expected to follow, Misail now despises the whole milieu in which his father lives and announces his intention of becoming a manual worker. This triggers off a predictable outrage in the old man and tears from his sister Cleopatra. He leaves home to find work on the railway for a time before joining his friend Radish who is a house painter.

---

[20] Ed. R. Hingley. *The Oxford Chekhov*. Vol. 8. p.7.

Meanwhile his sister has fallen for a young army doctor Blagovo, and, on one of their visits to Misail, the doctor shakes him by the hand saying that he much respects him for having the strength of character to live up to his beliefs but asks whether, if he had put all that effort into something more productive, such as turning himself into a scholar or an artist, it would have 'given his life greater depth and scope and made it more productive in every way.'

To this Misail protests with true Tolstoyan fervour:

> 'The strong must not enslave the weak and the minority must not be parasites on the majority or vampires for ever sucking their blood. In fact everyone without exception, strong and weak, rich and poor, should do his bit equally in the struggle for existence.'
> 'So your idea is that every single person should do manual work,' said the doctor.
> 'Yes.'
> 'Well, let's suppose all of us, including the elite and thinkers and great scholars play our part in the struggle for existence and spend our time breaking stones or painting roofs. Don't you think that might be a threat to progress?'
> 'Where's the threat?' I asked. 'Surely progress consists in good works and obeying the moral law.... If you stop making your neighbour feed and clothe you, carry you about and defend you from your enemies, surely that is progress in the context of a life built on slavery.'

Tolstoy is not mentioned by name but the arguments and even the tone of voice are unmistakable. In Blagovo's reply on the other hand one can hear Chekhov himself speaking.

> 'Have it your own way, but my ignorance is less of a bore than your knowledge. I'm climbing a ladder called progress, civilization, culture. I'm going higher and higher and don't know exactly where I'm heading, but really, this wonderful ladder alone makes life worth living. Now, you know what you're living for. You want one lot of people to stop enslaving another, you want the artist and the man who mixes his colours to eat the same food. But that side of life is so dim and commonplace, can't you see? Can't you see it's disgusting to live for that alone?'

The clash in ideological positions between Tolstoy and Chekhov is decisive. For Tolstoy, progress was moral progress or it was nothing. That was the core of life. It had been discovered once and for all and, besides this, scientific gadgets were irrelevant. Inventions had done nothing to solve the fundamental injustices in society. In some ways they had made the problem worse by giving the rich ever more efficient tools for oppressing the poor. Civilization, culture, refinement, most of medicine, as these existed in his day, only applied to the small elite who rode on the back of the majority. Slavery had been abolished but it still existed in practice and was justified by appeals to the 'scientific' theories of *laissez-faire* economics. Only by everyone sharing in the physical struggle of life could this appalling slavery be abolished.

Chekhov recognised the injustices in society. He was the grandson of a peasant, and had lived for years in the poorest quarters of Moscow that had so shocked Tolstoy. He worked in close contact with his peasant patients at Melikhova and with the prisoners on Sakhalin. But he was convinced that only by the application of reason and science could these great burdens on the poor be lifted. Unlike religious conversion, this could not be done in a flash. It would require generations of effort and the results would not be seen, at least on the scale of society as a whole, by those who were working to bring them about.

As the story of *My Life* unfolds Misail falls in love with the daughter of the railway engineer who gave him his first job and they get married. Masha is at first very influenced by Misail's Tolstoyism and they buy a large house in the country where he labours as a farmer while she builds a village school for the peasants. But any sentimental ideas about an idyllic country life are rudely shattered by the realities. The peasants, far from being noble savages, turn out to be cheats and swindlers when they are not drunk. Masha is disillusioned.

> We've done a lot of work, a lot of thinking. We're better for it.....
> but has our progress had any noticeable effect on the life around
> us? Has it done anyone else any good? No; ignorance, physical
> uncleanliness, drunkenness and the appallingly high infant mortality
> rate. None of that has changed. You've ploughed and sowed while
> I've spent money and read books, but what good has that been to
> anyone? All our work, all our fine ideals have clearly been only
> for ourselves.

Masha leaves her husband and eventually writes to him to ask him to

release her from their marriage so that she can devote her life to singing.
Misail returns to house painting in his home town, rejoining his sister
Cleopatra, who has also been deserted by Dr Blagovo, but who is now
pregnant. Shortly after this Cleopatra dies and at the close of the story
we leave Misail, a lonely and rather pathetic figure, visiting her grave
some years later with her daughter. As in *The Artist's Story*, it is impossible
to argue from the personal morality of the characters as we see it to the
validity of their ideas, or even to the wider value of their conduct. The
world is too complex for such equations to be valid. Dr Blagovo goes
abroad to work on vaccines for typhus and cholera, perhaps contributing
to the saving of countless lives in the future. Who can tell?

Did Chekhov have a greater capacity to tolerate uncertainty than
Tolstoy? In one of his great masterpieces, *The Lady with the Lapdog* he
treats his adulterous heroine without any of the implied disapproval that
we find in Anna Karenina. Like a good doctor, he understands that there
are no simple answers to the tragic situation in which she finds herself,
only a sensitively described dilemma. We are not called on to judge, only
to understand. When Tolstoy read the story he disapproved: 'All that
comes of reading Nietzche, and people who have no clear-cut views of
the world to help them to distinguish good from evil.'[21]

Maxim Gorki describes the two writers meeting in Yalta towards the
end of Chekhov's life. Tolstoy said to Gorki in a whisper: 'Ah, what a
dear, beautiful man, he is modest and quiet just like a girl. And he walks
like a girl. He's simply wonderful.' Then turning to Chekhov he asked:
'Did you fuck a lot of whores in your youth?'[22] Chekhov mumbled
something under his breath. He knew that he could not compete with the
sage of Yasnaya Polyana in that line of country.

---

[21] Henry Heim and Simon Karlinsky. *Anton Chekhov's Life and Thought*. University of California
Press. 1973. p. 375
[22] Maxim Gorki . *Reminiscences of Tolstoy*. 1920.

CHAPTER VI

The Country Doctor

On his return from Sakhalin, Chekhov joined his family once more in Moscow, but he did not take up his medical practice straight away. Most of the patients had presumably found other assistance in his absence and he may not have felt well enough to undertake professional work. His letters frequently refer to his own symptoms; continuous coughing, attacks of worrying palpitations and painful haemorrhoids which were to continue to plague him for the rest of his life. He went back to writing, however, making preliminary sketches for his story *The Duel*, and was besieged by would-be literary friends who wanted to invite the writer to their soirées and hear about his experiences in Asia. Chekhov found these requests tiresome, and once the winter was receding decided to set out on another journey, this time westwards to see the cities of Europe. He left Moscow in March 1891, travelling in the luxury coach of the International Society of Sleeping Cars to Vienna where he was delighted to find a complete absence of censorship, evident in the bookshops. For the next few months he did the grand tour, entranced with the splendours of Venice and Naples where he dragged himself up Vesuvius and peered over into the crater, ankle deep in ash. He spent a week in Nice, losing heavily at the casino and stayed over Easter in Paris before returning home.

Back in Moscow there was increasing alarm at the signs of impending famine in the countryside. The severe winter of the previous year had been followed by a very dry summer and there was consequent crop failure, especially in the central 'black earth' provinces of the Ukraine, usually the most prosperous of the country's agricultural regions. Since the emancipation of the serfs by Alexander II in 1861 the condition of the Russian countryside had progressively deteriorated. Peasants, who before that date had worked on the land of their masters were impoverished at having to buy the land they worked. The administration of the villages was in the hands of the Mir, a council of village workers, who parcelled out the available land in small strips that were difficult to work efficiently, and hardly produced enough food to feed the family. The population of the countryside moreover was steadily increasing. Then, in the late eighties there was a world-wide agricultural crisis and the price of grain collapsed. Savage fiscal policies were adopted by the central government, in the person of the Minister of Finance, Vyshnegradskii, which bore very heavily on the peasants. Taxes were increased and grain was exported in large amounts in a desperate attempt to balance the budget. There were no grain reserves to meet the year of bad harvest and the cumulative effect on the peasant economy was to reduce the average householder to penury and near starvation.

By the autumn of 1891, golodnye kleb or famine bread was beginning to find its way onto many tables. This was made with rye adulterated with goosefoot, a weed of no nutritional value and liable to lead to diarrhoea and further protein loss. Some of the stricken farmers made desperate attempts to extend the amount of soil under cultivation by ploughing up the arable land, diminishing the area available for grazing and thus reducing the soil fertility further. Many of the able-bodied men were leaving the country and swelling the number of unemployed seeking work in the cities. As hunger and cold began to tighten their grip, some of the affected villages in the Ukraine started to sell their animals to feed their inhabitants. Thatch from houses was torn down for fodder or fuel. There were reports of mothers murdering their children to save them from the pains of hunger. Chekhov immediately made plans to visit one of the areas that was most severely affected, Nizni Novgorod on the Volga where he had an acquaintance from his first hospital post, a former army officer and now a 'land captain', Yevgraf Yegorov. At the last minute another attack of chest symptoms forced him to cancel the proposed visit and he had to be content with raising funds for a scheme which Yegorov had devised for buying the animals which the peasants were selling, feeding them during the winter and returning them to the owners the following Spring in time for the ploughing season. In a letter to Yegorov on December 11[1] Chekhov explained that people were increasingly reluctant to give donations to the government relief agencies or to the Moscow Red Cross on account of the stories of misappropriation of funds and wastage. Durnava, the Minister of the Interior, a bureaucrat

---

[1] A. Chekhov. Letter to Yevgraf Yegorov. 11 December 1891.

to his fingertips, was determined that all aid to famine victims should be channelled through either the Red Cross or the Ministry of Church Affairs. 'It takes the courage of a Tolstoy' Chekhov wrote ' to act in defiance of all prohibitions and do what duty demands.' The lack of reliable information about the real state of affairs in the country districts and the poor quality of the newspaper reports made it difficult for those concerned to know how serious the situation was. The enormous distances meant that distribution of food, then as now, was a major problem in Russia. He agreed, however, to publish an appeal for subscribers to help with Yegorov's plan.

In January Chekhov felt well enough to visit Nizni Novgorod and saw for himself the plight of the starving peasants. He paid a call on the Governor, Baranov, and spent a whole afternoon discussing the situation with him. Graf Baranov was one of the more energetic of the provincial governors who had foreseen the famine coming early in 1891 and mobilised relief grain supplies, keeping the government well informed of the situation. He had also, in common with many energetic men, little patience with bureaucratic procedures and antagonised the local zemtsvo by insisting that the control of the entire relief operation be left in his hands.

Chekhov was impressed by what was being done but the size of the problem was immense.

> In my presence fifty four poods of dried bread arrived from St Petersburg for twenty thousand people. The philanthropists would feed five thousand people with five loaves as in the Gospel.[2]

One day he narrowly escaped injury when the sledge in which he was travelling lost its way in a snowstorm and was buried in the snow. In the following month he set out again, this time to Varonyezh, in the company of Suvorin. Unfortunately the presence of his distinguished companion turned the journey into a series of celebratory dinners, all the civic dignatories emulating one another in their hospitality. He managed to find out how the horse project was working in this province and wrote to Yegorov that the governor, Kurovsky, had already bought about 400 horses which he immediately gave to other peasants in famine areas, instructing them to use the animals to transport grain. By this means it

---

[2] A. Chekhov. Letter to A.S. Suvorin. 22 January 1892.

was hoped that the peasants would earn enough money to buy their animals back again in the spring. Grain was being distributed he noted, and also portable ovens and coal. Despite the relief measures he observed families with five children who had had nothing to eat for five days. There had been attempts to set up soup kitchens in the manner of Tolstoy, but these had failed.

Volunteer relief workers come under scrutiny in one of Chekhov's stories *My Wife* which he wrote in this year, 1891. He described the mixed motives of the landowner and his wife who feel uneasy and guilty at the plight of the peasants; but this does not produce any effective action. They are far more concerned over their own unhappiness and their strained relationship. Despite the committee that the wife assembles in their house, the little relief work that is accomplished can hardly make any difference to the situation. One is left at the end of the story with an impression of the impotence of all this effort and ultimately of selfishness masquerading as philanthropy.

To what extent Chekhov was drawn to help the peasants by these experiences it is difficult to say. He resolutely avoids attributing altruistic motives to himself. He started looking for a suitable house in the country, however, and by February he found what he was looking for. He wrote to his brother Alexander:

> Now pay attention. The estate has been purchased in the Serpukhov district, a dozen miles from the railway station of Lopashnaya. Be impressed: 575 acres, 432 of them wooded, two ponds, a horrid stream, a new house, an orchard, a piano, three horses, a cow, a racing tarantass, a light trap, carts, a sledge, hotbeds, two dogs, birdhouses for starlings and other items too numerous for your fireman's mind to comprehend.[3]

The village of Melikhova where the house was situated lies about fifty miles south of Moscow. It was to be his home for the next seven years and the place where he most consistently practiced as a doctor. At the stage of buying the house he had never even seen it and when he first visited Melikhova it was entirely covered with snow. He was somewhat aghast at his own foolhardiness.

---

[3] A. Chekhov. Letter to A.P. Chekhov. 23 February 1892.

The village of Melikhova covered with snow. Chekhov is the figure in the foreground.

I've bought myself an estate

he wrote to a friend Lydia Avilova.

> In one or two years it will be sold at auction as I've bought it by a transference of bank debts. That's how foolish I've been.[4]

However, as the snow thawed, so did he, and on the 5th of March he was writing to his younger brother Ivan,[5]

> Herewith a decree for you from the landowning 'Lords'. Bring a plane, a brush for cleaning horses, a saddle of beef and twenty pounds of rye bread. The impression I get is an excellent one and I feel as I've not felt for a long time. Today, all day long, they've been throwing snow on the pond. In the rooms it's warm but fumy. My study has acquired a very pleasant appearance. Tomorrow I'm starting work. Keep well, and bring some corks, the ordinary bottle ones, and some pharmacists ones but not too many

and there follows two drawings of corks.

He turned straight away to the practice of medicine. When Ivan and his supplies arrived he was already working. His other brother Michael remembers those days in his biographical notes:

---

[4] A. Chekhov. Letter to L.A. Avilova. 29 April 1892.
[5] A. Chekhov. Letter to I.P. Chekhov. 5 March 1892.

From the first days that we moved to Melikhova patients began to arrive from 25-50 versts away. They came on foot, they brought them on carts and called Anton to visit them too from long distances. From very early in the morning women and children stood at his door waiting for medical help. He went out and listened to their complaints, examined them and dispensed advice or medicine. His constant assistant was his sister Marya. Expenses for medicines were considerable since he had to keep a whole dispensary in the house. And in the evenings they wrote up the case notes.[6]

He did not charge for the medicine however. Grateful patients thanked him by making presents of a pig or six pairs of gloves. By April 6th he could write to Suvorin

I have the muzhiks and shopkeepers under my thumb. I've conquered them. One had a haemorrhage from the throat, another had his arm crushed by a tree and a third had a sick little girl. I turned out to be their last hope. They bow'd to me respectfully like Germans to their pastor. I treat them kindly and all is well.

The area for which he had responsibility had 26 villages, 7 factories and one monastery. In the spring floods and in the autumn many of these villages were difficult to reach and needed long and exhausting journeys.

I have to be doctor and sanitary officer all rolled into one

he wrote in July.

My horses and carriages are all mangy. I don't know the way. In the evenings I can't see where I'm going and I haven't any money in my pocket..... I quickly get exhausted. There are some days when I have to go out four or five times.[7]

Later that month there was news of an impending cholera epidemic and the zemstvo asked Chekhov to be the medical officer for his district.

---

[6] E.B. Meve. *op.cit*. Chapter 4.
[7] A. Chekhov. Letter to A.S. Suvorin. 6 April 1892.

Chekhov's house in Melikhova.

The head of the Serpukhov district was, he found, a friend of his, Kurkine. He had known Chekhov as a medical student at Moscow and at his first hospital post, before joining the zemstvo as a sectional medical officer. Chekhov opted not to be paid for his work as it helped him to preserve 'in however small degree, my freedom of action', but he was in no sense hostile to the movement which had transformed medical care in the countryside.

The zemstvo system dated back twenty five years to the formation of district councils under Czar Nicholas II. Representatives were elected by three electoral colleges; rural landowners, urban property owners and peasant villages. The government had not intended the reforms to address medical and social needs but as a means of modernising the countryside and bringing economic prosperity to banks, factories and railways.[8] Health and education were in the beginning regarded as optional extras, but this aspect of their work gradually took over and in the sphere of medicine initiated what was to be, in effect, the first attempt at a national health service free at the point of delivery. Prior to this, medical care in the Russian countryside had been almost non-existent.

---

[8] I.I. Molleson. *Zemskaia Meditsina*. Moscow. 1871.

The doctors lived by and large in the towns and the peasants had to have recourse to feldschers, half trained medical assistants, or rely on folk remedies. A report issued by the Ministry of the Interior in 1877 acknowledged that Russia's death rate was higher than in other civilised states. Less than half the children born twenty years before were surviving at that date.[9]

Many of the doctors qualifying in the later 19th century went to the countryside in a spirit of idealism to work for the zemstvo. 'We medical students realised that the training and knowledge that we possessed were paid for by taxes from the people' said one doctor looking back on the seventies. 'We know that it was our duty during our careers to repay what we owed'[10]. The work was hard and not well paid, many of the district dispensaries were poorly stocked and the peasants were at first suspicious of the doctors. Gradually however the peasants were won over and the doctors banded themselves together to form societies in order to promote their cause. The most important of these, the Pirogov Society, founded in 1885 and named after a great Russian surgeon, became the focal point for bringing pressure on the government to support adequate medical services. The congresses of the Society were forums for progressive opinion and, in the face of increased retrenchment by St Petersburg, it became steadily more politicised until, on the eve of the 1905 revolution, the Society was banned for subversive activities.

The Serpukhov District in which Chekhov's village was situated was part of the Moscow Provincial Zemstvo, one of the most thriving and forward looking in the country, thanks to two individuals; its secretary Egrav Osipov, who became an opinion former in the Pirogov Society, and Erismann the professor of public health that Chekhov had encountered at the Medical School.

> Never had the Russian peasants been told that it was not inevitable that half their children should die before they reached the age of five, and the fact that thousands of rural peasants chose to travel long distances for medical help indicates that they were receptive to the idea that science could be used to counteract the threatening forces of nature. Thus writes one student of the changes[11].

---

[9] P. Krug. *Doctors and the Administration of Russian zemstvo Medicine*. 1864-85. p.1.

[10] A.P. Voskensenskii. Iz *vospominanii o polovekorom proshlom*. Vol. 1. p.24.

[11] P. Krug. *op.cit*. p.184.

For Osipov:

> The most important characteristic of zemstvo medicine is that it is
> a public organisation in which the doctor receives a definite salary
> from the zemstvo, and therefore does not need to have private
> financial dealings with individual patients. Note that this is not
> done with any idea of charity but as a direct and natural duty of
> society to its sick members[12].

The difficulty in the way of treating the peasants is vividly illustrated
by the cholera outbreak in 1891 in which Chekhov was actively involved.
The epidemic started in the port of Astrakhan at the mouth of the Volga,
where 4,499 cholera victims were recorded between 14th of June and
31st of July. Seventy percent had proved fatal.[13] This naturally terrified
the peasants and all sorts of superstitions were spread about. The nature
of the illness encouraged stories. The distinction between the living who
looked like corpses and the dead who were said to have muscle spasms
in the limbs up to forty minutes after all other signs of life had vanished,
was blurred. There were tales of people being buried alive. The priests
said that the outbreak was the result of sinfulness and organised processions
of the icons round the households spreading the infection further. One
popular rumour was that the government had organised the epidemic to
limit the population and their agents were obviously these new zemstvo
doctors. Wherever they went cholera seemed to follow. And their
insistence on burying the corpses in quicklime was obviously to hide the
evidence. A mob invaded the cholera barracks that had been hastily
improvised, 'rescued' the patients and burnt the building to the ground.
Thousands of patients and relatives took to the road pursued by the troops
and spread the disease to towns further up the river. Meanwhile in the
port hundreds of ships were ordered to stand off and put in quarantine.
They were left there for days and slowly food and water ran out. Then
a government steamer drew up and relief seemed to be in sight. It
unloaded on the wharf and was found to have nothing on board but
coffins.The most savage attack on a doctor was perpetrated in the
province of Saratov where a certain Doctor Molchanov, who was
employed by the zemstvo as a temporary physician in the town of

---

[12] E.B. Meve. *op.cit.* Chapter 4.
[13] N. Frieden. *op.cit.* pp.144-151.

Khalynsk, was preparing a local building for cholera victims. There had been considerable disquiet amongst the people and on June 30th it erupted. *The Physician*, the foremost Russian medical journal, gave the details of what happened as follows:[14]

> Tuesday, June 30th. The rumours and rumblings among the people
> intensified. A crowd of ruffians gathered, shouting and looking
> for members of the Sanitary Commission and the City Council,
> and for the physicians. Part of the crowd headed for the barracks
> to find Doctor Molchanov. But he had galloped off on horseback.....
> finding the riot at its height he stopped at the home of Count B.
> Apparently some street urchins told the crowd of his refuge and the
> mob headed for Count B's home, arriving just as Molchanov came
> out. They hurled themselves at him beating him without mercy
> and then went off to look for some other vicitms, when suddenly
> Molchanov raised himself slightly. The crowd hurled themselves
> on him again, beating him and dragging him around, raising him
> in the air and throwing him on the roadway. Having butchered him
> beyond recognition the murderers tossed him aside and left to
> menace others, leaving some of their number around the corpse
> who would not allow the body to be moved or covered. Peasant
> women spat on his face and railed at his imagined crimes.

After atrocities such as this it is not surprising that the doctors who volunteered to help were reluctant to be seen as official employees of the zemstvo. One physician recounted that his wife had enquired of some peasants why they trusted her husband during the epidemic and was told, 'But he is free, not a government physician. What interest has he in killing people?' This was probably Chekhov's reason for not wanting to be seen accepting pay from the zemstvo. However, he threw himself into the preparations with great thoroughness and for some months all thought of literary pursuits had to be put on one side.

> Now I am riding around, visiting villages and factories and
> gathering material for a medical convention. In 1848 cholera was
> widespread in my district: we estimate this time that it will be no
> less severe although, naturally, God disposes. The districts are

---

[14] Vrach. 1892. 29. 742.

extensive so that the physicians will be spending all their time in exhausting drives merely to get from place to place. There are no barracks; the tragedies will be played out in the huts or in the open air. There are no assistants. The promises of disinfectants and drugs are unlimited. The roads are abominable and my horses even worse. As for my health, already by noon I begin to feel fatigued and a desire to get to bed. That's without the cholera but what things will be like when it arrives we will soon find out.[15]

His financial position after buying the house was insecure and he worried about not being able to write.

Aside from this epidemic, I expect an epidemic of another disease which will inevitably attack my farmstead. It's impecuniousness. With the cessation of my literary work my income ceased as well. Without counting the three roubles fee received today from a patient with gonorrhoea my income is exactly nil.

Writing to a sister of a woman doctor who had been assigned to a neighbouring district he warned her of what she must expect.

Yelena Mikkailovna will be confronted with having to organise her section. Her patience will be very sorely tried since our zemstvo is noted for its dilatoriness and has saddled the doctors with all the heavy work of organisation. I am as furious as a chained watchdog. I have twenty-three villages and yet so far I haven't even a cot and will probably never get the medical assistant I was promised by the medical council. I drive from factory to factory begging as if for alms for premises to shelter my future patients. From morning until evening I am driving about and I'm already exhausted although the cholera hasn't yet appeared. Last evening I was soaked by a downpour, slept away from home, went home on foot swearing all the time. My laziness has been profoundly mortified.[16]

He was given authority to requisition huts and hire as many local assistants as was thought necessary and, in serious circumstances, could

---

[15] A. Chekhov. Letter to N.A. Leikin. 13 July 1892.
[16] A. Chekhov. Letter to N. Lintvaryova. 22 July 1892.

order a medical team from Moscow. The zemstvo were matching up to the emergency.

> The zemstvo workers here are educated.
> Colleagues are efficient, knowledgeable people; while the peasants have become so used to medicine that it will be hardly necessary to convince them that we physicians are not to blame for the cholera. In all probability they will not beat us up.

The treatment regimen that Chekhov advised for patients is given later in the same letter.

> If anyone in your estate should get cholera, give him naphthalene at the very beginning. If a person has a strong constitution you can give it to him with calomel or castor oil. It dissolves in the latter. Give him up to ten grains. Here is the treatment we have decided upon: first naphthalene, then applying the Cantani method: that is large tannin enemas at 40 degrees and subcutaneous injections of a solution of table salt. In addition I will be keeping the patients warm in every possible way, (hot coffee with cognac, hot pads, hot baths and so on) and in the early stages I will supplement the naphthalene with santonni which has a direct effect on intestinal parasites. The santonni method was my own idea.

And again:

> The enemas have a wonderful effect. They warm the patient up and they calm down the diarrhoea. The injections sometimes produce miracles but sometimes they paralyse the heart...[17]

Equipment however, was slow in coming. He wrote later in the month,

> Cholera will strike any day now and the zemstvo is just beginning to send to Berlin for Cantani syringes and even for Esmarch dishes. I have only one dish for twentyfive villages, not a single thermometer, only a pound of carbolic acid. Your sister is

---

[17] A. Chekhov. Letter to A.S. Suvorin. 1 August 1892.

probably better off. Blessed are the doctors who live in their
hospitals. We clinic organisers always feel impoverished and
alone. I have shelters at two factories; one is excellent, the other
is poor; there are some smaller shelters in the villages. All this I've
managed to acquire by begging from local residents. I haven't yet
spent a kopek of the zemstvo money. None of this is of importance
of course, and I can only assume that in a week's time the domains
of the King of the Medes will be ready to welcome the Indian
commas.[18]

The Indian commas were the cholera vibrio which had been isolated
by Robert Koch in India in 1883. The Cantani injections recognised the
importance of sodium depletion in cholera deaths and were a major
advance, being supplanted by intravenous therapy in the early years of
the twentieth century.

By the middle of August, Chekhov tells Suvorin that he is prepared
for the epidemic having 'two splendid barracks, with all equipment and
about five not splendid, but abominable.'[19] He has relieved the zemstvo
of the expenses of most of his supplies by begging them from local
factory owners. In Nizni Novgorod the disease had arrived and he took
great pride in the achievements of modern medicine.

> In Nizhni physicians and people of culture worked wonders,

he wrote to Suvorin.

> I was wild with rapture on reading about the cholera. In the good
> old days when thousands sickened and died, men could not so
> much as dream of the overwhelming victories that are now being
> achieved before our eyes. It is a pity that you aren't a physician and
> cannot share my satisfaction; that is to say truly feel and realise and
> understand all that is being done.

The enthusiasm for scientific medicine is characteristic of Chekhov.
He sometimes treats his medical work as self-evidently valuable whilst
his literature was done out of self-indulgence, or justified by bringing

---

[18] A. Chekhov. Letter to N. Lintvarova. 31 July 1892.
[19] A. Chekhov. Letter to A.S. Suvorin. 16 August 1892.

him in an income. He is delighted at the news that the great German pathologist Virchow has visited St Petersburg.

At other times, however, it was difficult to maintain his enthusiasm in the face of the never-ending calls on him from patients and the zemstvo work. Chekhovian comedies would occasionally be enacted in real life. He was called to the house of a neighbouring count, a millionaire, to see his wife whom he found with enormous diamonds in her ears and wearing a bustle. He says that she had no idea how to behave but resisted the impulse which he felt ('that stupid simmering feeling') to give her a good telling off. Instead he made a note of the ostentatious wealth and decided to tap them for assistance for his cholera programme. He returned one afternoon to interview the lady but found himself treated like a hired hand who had come looking for a job. She and her friend the Archimandrite of the nearby monastery said that they could not possibly help with accommodation. Chekhov asked them what they would do with those who were taken ill in the house and monastery. Oh, they explained, we are all well enough off here to pay for private medicine. At this the good doctor swore and lied like a trooper, claiming that he was so rich that money was no object to him either. He was only interested in what happened to his patients. He had to leave however without so much as a kopek from the lady. Shortly after this the count and countess decamped to Biarritz to escape the infection.

Fortunately the cholera epidemic did not extend as far as Melikhova and, by the middle of October, Chekhov was able to wind up his section, close the barracks and dismiss his assistants.

> It is winter. My area is already closed down, but the sick still visit me.... Lately I treated an old man for his headaches. He walked about bent double and moaning terribly. His migraines lasted about four days..... A countrywoman comes to see me, Avdotia, who has had a continuous headache lasting for a year. When it gets worse she lies in bed half conscious and weak with a horrible pulse and looks exactly like a typhus patient. Salicylates help her and in order to receive one or two powders she walks five versts to see me. I give her potassium iodide. That helps her too. In general potassium iodide is a splendid thing. Near us there have already been eleven cholera patients. This is the start. The real thing will come in the Spring. My area has been fortunate in as much as there was a doctor and an orderly, two splendid barracks, outpatients were received, visits to patients were made in the proper way,

PHOTO LEFT

Chekhov at Melikhova during the cholera epidemic of 1892.

reports were sent to the Health Committee but very little money was spent, viz 110 roubles and 76 kopeks. The lion's share of the expenditure I collected off my neighbours, the factory owners, who were being milked instead of the zemstvo. During this summer I have become such a hand at curing diarrhoea, vomiting and other horrid things that I am overjoyed.[20]

He felt more at home in the countryside than the town. The peasants trusted him. He had presided at the Medical Council of the zemstvo, visited the factories with Doctor Kurkine, and was well known to the other officials who stayed with him when passing through Melikhova. He made a report to the zemstvo on the year's work[21] in which he had seen 453 patients at the centre and made 576 house-calls between 21st July and 13th December. He apologised for his lack of skill in collecting statistics. These numbers did not represent the whole of the sick of the district as those needing surgical attention or admission to hospital did not fall under his care but he points out that 'the hospitals are too spread out to serve the needs of the population.' At the subsequent meeting of the zemstvo a formal proposition was proposed by the chairman 'thanking Dr A.P. Chekhov for his unselfish and useful part in the struggle against the threatening cholera epidemic in the Serpukhov District.'

During 1893 patients continued to come to Melikhova. His letters are full of references to the conditions;

my head has been aching for two days now. I have just come back from a factory to which I drove through the mud in a trap and where I examined the sick. In the morning I went by cart to an infant who had diarrhoea and vomiting. Medicine is exhausting and trivial to the point of vulgarity....... you return from Krukov and a messenger from Vaskimo is already waiting in the courtyard, and peasant women with infants overpower me. In September I give up medical practice for good.

On another occasion he reports:

Last night soaked in a downpour, slept out and in the morning tramped home in the mud.

---

[20] A. Chekhov. Letter to A.S. Suvorin. 18 October 1892.
[21] V.V. Khizniakov. *op.cit.* Appendix. p.128.

His sister Marya explains that her Chekhov

> sometimes frowned when they came for him when he was ill or
> very tired. But once we helped our brother to dress his frown
> disappeared and the man waiting in the porch could not see any
> sign of discontent on his face.[22]

Despite the frustration he had really no intention of giving up
medicine. He was becoming a legend in the area. Telepkina Kupernik,
the novelist, wrote anxiously from Moscow to enquire about the health
of her former wet nurse, who lived in Lopasnaya not far from Melikhova.

> You don't need to worry, my dear. We have a doctor near here the
> like of whom you won't find in Moscow. Six versts from here he
> is, Doctor Anton Pavlovitch, and he is well loved by everyone. He
> doesn't even charge me for my medicine.[23]

Another patient's reaction is related by M.D. Teleshev.

> I remember a casual conversation with an old man, a peasant from
> Lopasnaya. He had been a silk winder. We sat together chatting
> in a railway carriage on the Kurski line. Hearing that he came from
> Lopasnaya I said that I had an acquaintance there.
> 'Who?'
> 'Doctor Chekhov'
> 'Ah, Anton Pavlich.' The old man smiled, clearly pleased about
> something but then said 'funny chap' and added more severely,
> with an air of disapproval.
> 'No sense.'
> 'Who has no sense?'
> 'Anton Pavlich. What do you think? My wife when she was old
> kept going to him for treatment. He cured her. Then I fell ill and
> he attended to me. I gave him money but he wouldn't take it. So
> I say 'Anton Pavlich, my dear chap, what are you doing? What are
> you going to live on? You're not stupid and you know your
> business.' I said 'Think of yourself. Where will you go if some
> day they dismiss you from the service? That could happen to

---

[22] E.B. Meve. *op.cit.* p.15.
[23] V.V. Khizniakov. *op.cit.* p.33.

anyone. You can't take to trade.' So he laughs and says 'If they chase me away I'll have to marry a wealthy woman merchant.' 'And who will marry you if you have no situation?' said I, 'but he just kept on laughing.'[24]

At first members of the family, his sister Marya and his brother Michael helped him, the latter preparing the ointments and mixing the medicines. Subsequently he employed a nurse assistant, Zinaida Vasilyevna. Brief letters have survived which give a glimpse of his medical practice:

> Dear Zinaida,
>   Could you please make arrangements for this female patient to be examined by Dr Oscar Ferdinandovitch. And afterwards write to me giving his opinion about the nature of her illness. Meanwhile give her Kaljodat 5.0 in parts 200.0, three teaspoonfuls a day. If Oscar F finds it necessary for her to have hospital treatment, could she be admitted to the Semenovskaya Hospital?
>   When are you coming to see us?
>   I wish you all the best.
>   A.Chekhov.

And on another occasion:

> Would you be so kind to give me on a loan basis 1/2 or 1/4 lb castor oil. I would be most grateful. I've bought for you in Paris a most beautiful umbrella. It will be arriving here any day. But if you don't come and visit us soon you won't get the umbrella. That's a threat. I would have sent a horse for you but our mare is in foal. They are always in foal!

During 1893 further cholera outbreaks meant that the business of requisitioning and preparing barracks had to be gone through once more. This time he found the factory owners more co-operative. A local peasant offered him a substantial building in one village and in another a pub was provisionally earmarked. On this occasion the zemstvo gave him a medical assistant to help with the work at a monthly salary of forty

---

[24] N. Teleshev. *Reminiscences*. 1943. pp.101-2.

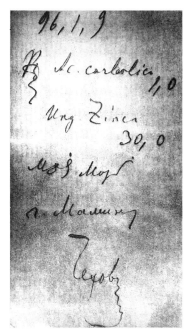

A Chekhov prescription.

roubles. In his annual report he records 498 'dispensary patients' having been seen in 1893 and 780 visits made which suggests quite an active medical life.[25]

Chekhov was often distressed at the sufferings of the sick. As he explained to Suvorin

> A doctor has terrible days and hours. I would not wish them on anyone. Among doctors, it is true that there are ignorant and rude people, as also among writers, engineers and people in general. But these terrible hours and days that I am speaking of only happen to doctors. And for that I say much will be forgiven them. A country wife was carting rye and tumbled head first off the cart. Smashed herself dreadfully. Concussion of the brain, strain of the neck muscles, vomiting and great pain and so on. They brought her to me. Moans and ohs and ahs. She implores God for death. Yet her eyes are fixed on the peasant who brought her in and she

---

[25] V.V. Khizniakov. op.cit. p.130.

mumbles: 'Have done with the lentils, Krylla, thresh them later but
get threshing the oats now.' I tell her that talk about oats could be
put off for really there is something of a more serious nature to talk
about, but she tells me 'He's got very good oats.' A bustling
greedy country wife. Such people find it easy to die.[26]

In May 1894 he described a visit to the congress of zemstvo doctors
from the whole of the Moscow district, which was held at the neighbouring
village of Pokrovskoie-Mescherskoie.

> Here in an old country house there is at present a zemstvo
> psychiatric hospital for the county. All the doctors of the district
> have assembled here - seventyfive of them, and I one of the
> number. There were large numbers of patients but most of the
> cases were subjects for the psychiatrist rather than the psychologist.
> One patient was preaching that the Holy Family came down on
> earth in the guise of the metropolitan Iounikyi. There is a time limit
> of ten years: eight years have already passed - two years remain.
> If we don't want the whole of Russia to blow up like Sodom we
> must all go in procession to Kiev...... He prays all the time with his
> face to the East and sings, addressing himself to God, never failing
> to add the words 'In the dignity of metropolitan Iounikyi'. The
> expression on his face is beautiful. I was coming home late from
> the madhouse in a troika. Two thirds of the journey took me
> through the forest with the moon shining, and my state of mind was
> extraordinary. I had not felt like that for a long time, as though I
> was returning from a tryst. I think that nearness to nature and
> idleness are the necessary elements for happiness: without them it
> is impossible.[27]

The letters are full of medical advice. To Suvorin who enquired about
dizzy attacks he replied.

> Swaying, reeling accompanied by dimness of vision or even loss
> of consciousness for a few seconds and also a feeling as though a
> wind or a hurricane is blowing through your head is a phenomenon
> that is almost usual in men of your age, with women of any age or

[26] A. Chekhov. Letter to A.S. Suvorin. 18 August 1891.
[27] A. Chekhov. Letter to A.S. Suvorin. 9 May 1894.

Chekhov's stethoscope (mon-aural)
and tendon hammer.

badly-nourished young people. One must come to terms with it.
Put it down to age. Don't walk too quickly when your brain is
working or when wearing a heavy overcoat. It is a common illness
in elderly peasants and I treat it by saying that they should not be
frightened and should not change their mode of life. In addition
I give them valerian, ten drops four times a day especially if the
pulse is weak. Every case is treated on its merits. A prolonged
conversation may attract blood to the lungs and therefore deprive
the brain and lead to weariness, so don't chatter so much and avoid
getting constipated.[28]

He finishes as usual with his tongue in his cheek. To his brother
Alexander who complained of a sore throat and a cough he wrote

the pharynx is a very sensitive part of the body and it soon gets used
to gargles and mouthwashes. The best way to stop catarrh is to give
up smoking, don't drink very hot liquids and don't breath dust-
polluted air.[29]

On the other hand he was critical of any attempt by imaginative
writers to use medical details in their stories for effect. Yelena Shavrova,
the author, asked Chekhov's opinion of a story concerning the effects of
syphilis.

---

[28] A. Chekhov. Letter to A.S. Suvorin. 17 October 1892.
[29] A. Chekhov. Letter to Alexander Chekhov. 3 October 1897.

To write about an illness or about degeneration, psychosis etc, the writer has to be scientifically acquainted with them. You exaggerate the importance of the illness, (out of modesty let us designate it with the capital 'S'). First S is curable, and secondly if the doctor finds that the patient has some serious illness, tabes or cirrhosis of the liver for instance, and if the condition is due to S then he is comparatively hopeful because it can be treated. Degeneration, nervousness and debility are not due to S alone, but to a combination of many factors, vodka, tobacco, the overeating in the intellectual classes, and appalling upbringing, lack of physical exercise, the conditions of city life and so on and so forth..... by the way, do you know that influenza also ravishes the organism in ways that are far from insignificant? There's very little in nature that isn't occasionally harmful.... Personally I keep to the following rule: I write about sickness only when it forms part of the characters or adds colour to them. I avoid terrifying my readers with illnesses. I do not accept that our century is a century of stress because people have been stressed in all ages. Anyone who is afraid of being stressed must turn himself into a sturgeon or a smelt.[30]

In 1895 Chekhov heard that one of the few Russian medical journals *The Surgical Chronicle* was threatened with closure through lack of funds. The loss would be critical for Russian medicine: 'A good surgery journal', he wrote, 'is as useful as performing twenty thousand operations.' He immediately set out to find another publisher, addressed letters to different publishing houses and went to solicit help from philanthropists but to no avail. He would have given the journal enough money himself to cover its deficit for the coming year but his finances were stretched to the limit by the building of a school at the nearby village of Talezh. Suvorin sent fifteen hundred roubles and eventually a publisher was found. However, now the authorities refused to sanction the appointment of the editor. Further difficulties continued through 1896 and occupied Chekhov in many visits to St Petersburg at the time when he was arranging for the première of his play *The Seagull*. At length in 1897 the *Surgical Chronicle* was established and started publishing regularly again. The following year the fortunes of the journal were augmented by a gift from the owner of one of the countries largest sugar refineries who

---

[30] A. Chekhov. Letter to I.J. Shavrova. 28 February 1893.

had just recovered from a successful operation. The new editor wrote to Chekhov:

> I've done so much damage to your sensibility with my complaints that I consider myself under an obligation to share with you as soon as possible a pleasant bit of news. You sympathised so much with me in this matter and supported me so well in my bitter disappointments that I have no doubt now that you rejoice in our success.[31]

As a writer, Chekhov felt he had a particular obligation to encourage other doctors to take up the pen in their professional interests and to use the national press to spread their ideas. To a neighbouring doctor he writes that:

> It is time that zemstvo doctors and other medical workers stopped turning up their noses at the press and behaving towards it as though it were their enemy. They should all join in newspaper controversies in their areas, especially the public health doctors who refuse to do this out of pride. I agree that sending items to a paper is a trifling matter but don't you see that life's made up of trivialities, penny pieces - but these soon mount up to pounds....! *Russian Lists* a few months ago dealt inaccurately with the question of Public Health Committees. It was not however *Russian Lists* that was to blame but the Public Health Committee members.[32]

Outside medicine Chekhov became extensively involved in the provision of schools for the peasants. The importance of education in the welfare of society was regarded by the progressive thinkers amongst zemstvo workers as critical. Many areas had no schools whatever and those that existed were very primitive. Chekhov had been appointed a schools inspector and had first-hand knowledge of these deficiencies. Reporting on the state of the school in the village of Kryukova, he was struck by the overcrowding, the low ceilings, the inefficient and depressing iron stove which stood in the middle of the classroom, old and poor furniture, coats hanging all over the classroom. In the small hall the school caretaker was asleep on some rags. Here too was a tub with the

---

[31] I.M. Guyzer. *Chekhov i Meditsina*. Moscow. 1954. p.21.
[32] V.V. Khizniakov. *op.cit.* p.127.

children's water, and the WC failed to satisfy even the most modest requirements of hygiene or aesthetics. The teachers in schools were miserably paid. At another village he noted that the teacher

> received only 23 roubles a month. He has a wife and four children
> and is already grey despite being only thirty. So cowed is he by
> need that, no matter what you may start talking to him about, he
> will bring the subject around to the problem of salary.[33]

During his stay at Melikhova Chekhov supervised and helped to finance no less than three schools for the peasants, first at Talesh, then at Novosyolki and finally at Melikhova. Raising funds for these enterprises found him and his sister Marya running bazaars, selling paintings donated by his friend Levitan and even organising local amateur performances. Chekhov himself designed the buildings and hired local workmen to erect them.

> All through Lent and then throughout April I shall again have to
> see to carpenters, caulkers and so on. Again I am building a school.
> A deputation from the muzhiks called on me with a request and I
> didn't have the heart to turn them down. The zemstvo's contribution
> is a thousand roubles, the muzhiks have collected three hundred
> and that's all, but the school will cost no less than three thousand
> which means that I shall again have to be thinking about money all
> summer long and snatching a bit here and a bit there. Life in the
> country is full of problems.[34]

Hingley points out in his biography that it is rather surprising, that with all this medical and social activity there is very little mention of it in the twenty seven stories that he wrote whilst living at Melikhova. A considerable number of doctors are portrayed in them but often in circumstances that were far removed from his own. However in one important story *Peasants* he not only gives a vivid and unflattering account of life in a peasant village but achieved a degree of notoriety in the process. Following the Slavophil beliefs, many of the intellectual elite romanticised the life of the peasants with whom they had little first-hand experience, regarding them as the soul of Holy Russia and as

---

[33] A. Chekhov. Letter to A.S. Suvorin. 27 November 1894.
[34] A. Chekhov. Letter to A.S. Suvorin. 8 February 1897.

embodying many simple rural virtues. Support for these ideas was even found in the writings of Tolstoy. When the new story appeared in *Russkaya Mysl - Russian Thought -* and the readers found an account of peasant life which was brutal, violent and sordid, there were immediate protests. During the summer and the winter they read 'there had been hours and days when these people seemed to live worse than beasts.' The censor refused to allow one page of the story in which it was stated that most of the peasants did not believe in God, and this was immediately excised. The son of the peasant family described in the story has returned to his home from Moscow because he has a serious disease. He and his wife witness the brawling and drunkenness of his relatives and neighbours. Eventually his mother invites a local 'feldscher', a retired medical orderly, to see her son. The peasants were credulous and ignorant in medical matters.

> They were always talking about colds, tapeworms and tumours going round the stomach and up to the heart. They were more frightened of 'catching cold' than of anything else so wrapped up well and warmed themselves on the stove even in the summer. The feldscher advises cupping, a practice that was already old fashioned and discredited. Twenty-four cups were put on the unfortunate patient. 'Nicholas started to shiver. His faced looked peaked and seemed 'clenched like a fist'. His fingers turned blue. He wrapped himself in a blanket and sheepskins but grew colder and colder. By evening he felt very low. He wanted to be put on the floor and asked the tailor not to smoke. Then he went quiet inside his sheepskin and by morning he was dead.

The dry, almost ironic tone of this description expresses with considerable force, the evil inherent in the system of medical assistants who in many areas were the only aid for the rural communities.

One of the principal criticisms voiced by the leading zemstvo doctors against the status quo was the reliance on feldschers. The word was derived from the German term 'field barber' or a 'field surgeon'. They had been introduced into the Russian army by Peter the Great and by the nineteenth century were the mainstay of medical care to the peasants.[35] In the Viatka province for instance in 1883 there were seven medical centres manned entirely by feldschers, each of them serving 30,000

---

[35] Peter Krug. *op.cit.*

people and covering an area of sixty five miles in diameter. Many of
them, as in Chekhov's story, had returned from army service. They were
dangerously ill-informed and frequently brutal, authoritarian and
alcoholic. In one of the early stories *An Unpleasant Incident* Chekhov
describes a hospital doctor slapping a feldscher on the face in front of the
patients for being drunk on duty. Later in the same story the doctor
discussed the problem.

> The in-between man as you call him is unreliable. We sack him,
> curse him, slap him in the face but we should really try to see things
> from his point of view too. He's neither peasant nor gentry, neither
> fish nor fowl. His past is bitter. His present is made up of a salary
> of twenty-five roubles a month, a hungry family and a subordinate
> position, which he will retain were he to stay in his job for a
> hundred years. He has no education and no property, no time to
> read and go to church and he can't even hear what we have to say
> because we don't let him get near us. And so he lives on from day
> to day until he dies, without a hope of a better future on a starvation
> diet, terrified of being thrown out of his free flat at any moment,
> not knowing where his children's next home will be. And this
> being so how can he possibly not take to drink or steal? You tell
> me that.

The problem continued to exercise Chekhov and he introduced
feldshers into many of his stories, such as *Ward Number Six*, *The Thieves*,
Rothchild's Fiddle, *Judgement* and *Grief*.
    1887 saw Chekhov still hard at work at his medical practice despite
rapidly failing health. In January he wrote to Suvorin:

> The fact is I am terribly busy. I've never had so much work as I
> have at the moment. It's difficult to tear myself away ..... As for
> outbreaks of the plague, whether it's coming or not nobody knows.
> If it does come then it's not all that alarming as both the patients
> and the doctors here have long been used to high mortality, thanks
> to diptheria, typhoid and so on. You see, even without the plague,
> scarcely 400 out of 1000 survive to reach the age of five and in the
> villages and in the cities, in the factories and the back streets you
> will not find even one healthy woman. The situation will be so
> much worse in that the plague may well come two or three months
> after the census. The people will interpret the census in their own

way and attack the doctors for poisoning the superfluous population to leave more land for the landowners. The quarantine measures are poor. The innoculations of Kutkin give some hope but in Russia, unfortunately, he is not popular. 'Christians have to beware of him as he is a Jew.'[36]

The census was the first to be undertaken in Imperial Russia and Chekhov immediately volunteered to help.

They've handed out some revolting ink pots, revoltingly ugly badges like those used in a brewery, and wallets into which the census sheets will not fit, like ill-fitting sabres in their sheaths. It's quite ridiculous. From dawn I wander about among the peasant huts and because I'm not used to them, bang my head on the door lintels and unfortunately my head aches hellishly. So I've a migraine and probably have influenza coming on. In one hut there is a little girl nine years of age that they've adopted from an institution, crying bitterly because all the other girls in the family in that hut are called Mikailovna but she's only known by the patronymic name Lynbov, after her godfather. I said to her 'You're to be called Mikailovna too.' Everybody cheers up wonderfully and they all started thanking me. That is what is called making yourself friends of the mammon of untruthfulness.[37]

In February this additional labour was thankfully over.

I got quite fed up with the whole business since I had to enumerate and write at the same time until I got writer's cramp. I also had to lecture to fifteen census takers. They did excellent work but were so pedantic as to be laughable. But the census supervisors from the zemstvo who were in charge of the rural districts behaved very badly. They did nothing, understood little, and during moments of the utmost difficulty took sick leave. The best one turned out to be a drunkard and a boaster like Khlestakov but at least he was a character and comic. The rest were colourless and it was a nuisance to have to associate with them.[38]

[36] A. Chekhov. Letter to A.S. Suvorin. 17 January 1897.
[37] A. Chekhov. Letter to A.S. Suvorin. 11 January 1897.
[38] A. Chekhov. Letter to A.S. Suvorin. 8 February 1897.

The effort of this extra work in the middle of winter can only have accelerated his underlying illness and in March 1897 this suddenly showed itself in an unmistakeable fashion. He was having dinner with his friend Suvorin in The Hermitage Restaurant in Moscow when he collapsed with a massive haemorrhage from the lungs. He was carried up to Suvorin's flat at the Slavyansky Bazaar where Nicolai Obolonsky, a doctor and a mutual friend, saw him and persuaded him to see Professor Ostroumov. From here he was admitted to the professor's ward at the central hospital, the diagnosis of extensive pulmonary tuberculosis could no longer be brushed under the carpet and from now onwards his life was to be very different.

CHAPTER VII

Astrov and Co: Some Chekhovian Doctors

> In order to live well as a human being one must work, work with
> love, believe in one's work, and here in Russia we don't know how
> to do this. A doctor if he is in practice no longer keeps up with
> science. He reads nothing except *News of Therapy*, and at the age
> of forty is seriously convinced that all diseases stem from cold.

This remark is attributed to Chekhov by Maxim Gorki in his
Reminiscences and certainly reflects the outlook on life of many doctors
to be found in his writings who seem to have succumbed to a sort of mid-
life crisis, losing their idealism, overeating and attributing all their ills to
the times in which they live. Michael Astrov, the doctor in Uncle Vanya
is, therefore, somewhat unusual in having many marks of the author's
approval in his character. He is a habitual hard worker, devoted to his
medical vocation among the peasants, as Chekhov was at Melikhova.
The Voinitsky household has, as he says towards the end of the play,
infected all with its idleness.

> I've been under your spell and I've done nothing for a whole
> month while all the time people have been falling ill and villagers
> have been grazing their cattle in my newly-planted woods.

The life of a rural doctor in the nineteenth century was hard and
unremitting, and required great physical and emotional stamina. As
Astrov relates to Marina, the old nurse:

> On my feet from morning to night with never a moment's peace,
> and then lying under the bedclothes afraid of being dragged out to
> a patient. All the time we've known each other I haven't had one
> day off.

He goes on to describe a patient who died on the operating table under his care.

> Then, at the worst possible moment, my feelings came to life and
> I felt as guilty as if I'd murdered the man.

Because doctors deal with life and death and cannot avoid errors of judgement they have to learn to live with their consciences. Chekhov is talking from his own experience. Working in extreme isolation he would have found himself called upon to deal with conditions that he knew were outside his competence. His brother Michael described how Anton tried to deal with a man who had eviscerated his abdomen on a hay fork, laying the patient down on the floor of his own study at Melikhova.[1] We are not told whether the patient recovered. The case of the daughter of the Yanov family who died from typhoid fever in his care we know troubled him to the point that he threatened to abandon medicine altogether.

Besides his devotion to medicine, Astrov shares another passion with his creator, his concern for the environment. He is absorbed in an astonishingly modern way with the threat posed by the destruction of Russia's forests and is a keen tree planter. These preoccupations are even more apparent in the character of Dr Michael Krushchov in *The Wood Demon*, a play which turned out to be a preliminary study for *Uncle Vanya*. Krushchov is a landowner with a medical degree and it is implied that he has no permanent post, Chekhov's situation at Melikhova. The idealisation of Krushchov, however, and the final act of the play in which all the psychological problems are resolved give *The Wood Demon* a didactic air that Chekhov was careful to remove in the transformation to *Uncle Vanya*. Astrov is made a morally ambiguous, but more interesting character, with a weakness for alcohol and beautiful women.

Coming from peasant stock himself, Chekhov seems to have found relationships easier with the peasants than with more aristocratic patients. Two stories describe angry confrontations between doctors and demanding members of the upper classes. In *Enemies* a hospital doctor, Kirillov, who has just seen his son die from diphtheria is immediately summoned by a landowner living a long distance away to visit his wife. Dr Kirillov protests that it is inhuman to ask him to go away from his own household

---

[1] V.V.Khizniakov. *op.cit.* Introduction.

on a dark September night, leaving his own distraught wife behind, but the landowner continues to harangue him until he agrees to go. When they arrive at the patient's house after a long journey, it is to find that the wife has run off with her lover and was obviously putting on a hysterical display to get rid of her husband. The landowner, instead of apologising, pours out his matrimonial troubles to the enraged doctor who at last loses his self control and shouts

> 'Why are you telling me all that? I refuse to listen to you. I refuse!', banging on the table with his fist. 'I have no use for your dirty secrets, damn them! How dare you tell these sordid things to me? Or do you think that I have not been insulted enough? I am a doctor, and you look upon doctors and workers in general who do not smell of perfume and prostitution as your lackeys and bad form. Well, look down on them all you want, but no one has given you the right to make a stage prop out of a man who's suffering.'

Another protest at the indignities suffered by doctors at the hands of their social superiors is found in *The Princess*. A member of the aristocracy is paying a visit to a monastery. She is a Lady Bountiful, always setting up situations that advertise her munificence but with a total failure to appreciate the real needs of others less fortunate than herself. On her visit, she meets an elderly doctor who had formerly been in her employment and, in a gushing mood, exclaims that she wishes to know all her faults. She is considerably surprised when this releases a torrent of criticism, accusing her of hypocrisy and pretence that continues for several pages. She has dismissed him without giving any reason....

> 'I'm a doctor of medicine and a gentleman' he shouts. 'I trained at Moscow University and am the father of a family - that is, I'm such a worm and a nonentity that I can be thrown out on my ear without any explanation.'

In nineteenth century England general practitioners felt at a social disadvantage when treating their middle and upper class patients. The situation in Russia, however, was much worse. V.F. Smigirev in a eulogy of Professor Zakharin given in 1898 says

> Who can forget how the doctor once stood in the doorway, afraid to take a seat? How some doctors were only allowed to treat

peasants, and others appeared like a watchmaker in a frock coat at an established hour to ask about the health of the master of the household?[2]

In a projected census of 1864 in St Petersburg physicians were in the section for artisans between porters, pianists and piano tuners on one side and typesetters on the other.[3] During the last half of the nineteenth century there was a determined attempt to improve the standing of the doctor by better medical education, the development of professional organisations, foremost among which was the Pirogov Society, and by the emergence of serious medical journalism. The achievements of scientific medicine in bringing relief to many disabling and fatal diseases also did much to enhance the prestige of the practitioners. Even poor doctors could cure diseases and relieve pain. Most of the doctors remained poorly paid however. Only handfuls of physicians in the city centres were able to make a reasonable living by private practice.

Many of the country practitioners, mostly employed as zemstvo physicians, were grossly overworked and the rough conditions of peasant life coarsened their characters. Dr Sable in the story *My Wife* is seen through the eyes of the landowner narrator and is typical.

> We heard the noise of Dr Sable's arrival. While he rubbed his cold hands and tidied his wet beard I had time to notice, firstly that he was bored with life, and therefore glad to see me and Bragin and secondly that he was a bit of a simpleton and an innocent. He looked at me as if I must be overjoyed and fascinated to see him. 'I haven't been to sleep for two nights' he said, gazing at me innocently and combing his beard. 'I spent the first night on a confinement and the next at a peasant's where I had bed-bugs biting me all night. I'm as tired as hell if you see what I mean.' With the air of one who could not fail to purvey pleasure unalloyed, he took my arm and led me to the dining room. His innocent eyes, crumpled frock coat and cheap tie, the smell of iodoform.... these things struck me disagreeably and made me think of him as a social inferior. '*Repetitio est mater studiorum*', said Sable, swiftly tossing down his second glass. 'I'm so glad to see such nice people, you

---

[2] V.F. Smigirev. *Pamiati Zakharina* published as introduction to *Zakharin G.A. Klinicheskie Lektsii*. Moscow. 1910. p.14.
[3] N. Frieden. *op.cit.*

know I don't feel tired any more. I've turned into a peasant. I've gone to seed out there in the back of beyond - run wild, I have. But I am still an intellectual, gentleman, and I can't stand the lack of social life I tell you straight.'

The story achieves remarkable psychological depth by using as a narrator a thoroughly unlikeable character. Asorin, the landowner, is a misanthropic domestic tyrant who, despite having separated from his wife, refuses to let her have a passport or lead an independent existence. He is morbidly jealous of her achievements and of her friends, and is absorbed most of the time in attempts to justify his own behaviour. As his wife says, and I think we can believe her, he has never performed a disinterested kindly act in his life. All Asorin's work for the famine is motivated by a similar self interest. He has no hesitation in getting detectives to hunt out the starving peasants who have been raiding his barns. We see Dr Sable through the distorting mirror of this man's perceptions. After contributing 500 roubles to the wife's fund for famine relief he tells her:

> Permit me one parting word of advice my dear. Do be careful with Sable and your helpers in general, don't confide in them. I don't say they are dishonest, but they aren't gentlemen. They have no ideas, these people. They lack ideals and faith. They are without any purpose in life or firm principles and their whole life revolves around money, money, money!

As poor old Sable has not even sufficient money to buy tobacco for himself this parting shot is a crowning injustice.

Being dragged out of bed to see sick patients was a particular trial for the country doctor. Chekhov writes in 1892 of the

> revolting days and hours which only doctors are subject to.... I feel sick at heart and fed up. Oh! Not to belong to oneself any longer. To spend one's time thinking only about diarrhoea, to start and tremble at night when the dogs bark and there's knocking at the gate. Have they come for me to go out on those uncharted roads?[4]

---

[4] V.V. Khizniakov. *op.cit.*

Such was the case with Dr Kirillov in *Enemies* and a similar situation is described in another early story, *The Mirror* but in this case the doctor is himself sick. An unmarried woman dreams of the husband she hopes to find, but the dream turns into a nightmare as her husband becomes seriously ill and she has to call the doctor. It is a cold night in winter and she knocks on the door of Dr Stepan Lukich. The cook who receives her says the doctor is ill in bed after returning from dealing with an epidemic illness. She impatiently brushes past the woman however, and searches through the house until she finds the doctor's bedroom. Despite his protests of being unable to work she drags him off to see her husband. By the time they reach the patient's house the doctor is too sick to be of any help and her husband dies. Bernard Shaw described the plight of the overworked industrial doctor in the preface to *The Doctor's Dilemma*.

> He may be hungry, weary, sleepy, run down by successive nights, disturbed by that instrument of torture the night bell; but who ever thinks of this in the face of sudden sickness or accidents? We think no more of the condition of the doctor attending a case than of a fireman attending a fire.

Such were the conditions under which most general medical practitioners in the nineteenth century worked, a situation that was only to begin to change in England with the advent of National Insurance schemes under Lloyd George. In Russia, zemstvo medicine had constructed a framework that could theoretically have delivered an effective medical care system to the peasants but the shortage of doctors was such that it was impossible to make any real contribution and the strain on those doctors who became zemstvo employees was so great that many cracked under it. Astrov and Sable had both taken to the bottle as a way of relieving their tensions. But they had not given up the struggle or become cynical in the process.

This could not be said of another group of doctors of which Dr Startsev, in the story of that name, may be taken as the representative. These failed professional figures have abandoned whatever scientific interest they once had in their work and pursue either money or their own comforts. Dorn in *The Seagull* and the pathetic army doctor in *The Three Sisters* are other members of this species. Dmitry Startsev had commenced his career as a country physician, spending most of his time at the local hospital. It is only after he has been invited to the odious family of the Turkins where he falls in love with Catherine, the daughter of the house, and following his ignominious rejection by this lady that his fall from grace begins. He moves into town and gathers a large private practice, driving round his patients ostentatiously in a troika with bells, and likes nothing better than counting the banknotes that he has acquired on his rounds. He becomes addicted to food so that he is too fat to walk with comfort and, instead of visiting the hospital, plays bridge three times a week. Worst of all, in Chekhov's scale of values, he loses his temper with the patients, shouting at them fiercely as he bangs his stick on the floor: 'Pray confine yourself to answering my questions. Less talk!' Chekhov was much fascinated by the problem of professional men who lost their youthful ideals in middle life, but strangely regarded this as a specifically Russian disease, putting it down to the corrupting effect of life in small provincial towns.

Two doctors found in the stories seem to be without flaws of any kind, to be in the class of medical saints, and, interestingly, neither portrait is quite convincing. *The Head Gardener's Story* is a Tolstoyan fable about a general practitioner who lives all his life in a small town, shunning social contacts, and surrounded with his books, but selflessly responding to calls for medical assistance, despite having pulmonary tuberculosis. He is worshipped by the inhabitants to such a degree that, when his body is discovered, accompanied by unmistakable evidence of his being been murdered, the community cannot believe that anyone could be motivated to kill him and the obvious suspect is released without punishment. As a moral fable this does not carry conviction and it is strange to find such a story comparatively late in Chekhov's career (1894), when he had ceased to be attracted by Tolstoy's philosophy. Could it be that Chekhov's humour is operating slyly here in that he is suggesting that the head gardener is naive to accept such an improbable story?

Osip Dymov, the doctor in *The Butterfly* is a different matter. Although this story is not quite in the front rank, it is interesting in contrasting two opposed attitudes to life. On the one hand there is the scientific man in the person of Dymov, working all day at the hospital, with no time for social contacts, having hardly any private patients, unlike Dr Startsev, and so only able to travel round town on a horse drawn tram. On the other we have his flighty wife Olga, and her bohemian friends. For Dymov the world of arts and artists is one that he cannot understand.....

'I don't understand them,' he tells his wife. 'I've worked at science and medicine all my life and I've no time to be interested in the arts.'

When she says that this attitude of his is awful he replies:

> Why so? Your friends know nothing of science and medicine, but
> you don't hold that against them. Everyone has his own line. I
> don't understand landscapes and operas, but if highly intelligent
> people give their whole lives to them and other intelligent people
> pay vast sums for them, then they must be important.

The husband and wife inhabit different worlds, the two cultures of
C.P. Snow. When Olga sails off to have an affair with a painter friend
this relationship quickly goes sour on them, and she returns to her
husband, uncontrite. It is only when he contracts a fatal attack of
diphtheria by aspirating a diphtheritic membrane from the throat of an
infected boy that she realizes what heroic stuff her unassuming Osip is
made of. After his death one of his medical colleagues drives home the
moral, pointing to her extravagant wardrobe.

> He served science, he died for science. He slaved away day in, day
> out, nobody spared him - and a young scholar, a budding professor,
> had to tout for private patients and spend his nights translating to
> pay for these disgusting rags!

If the saintly Dymov somewhat undermines the credibility of the
story, Chekhov draws a telling contrast between the self-centred and
loquacious lives of many artists of his acquaintance and the ideal of the
disinterested pursuit of science. The story roused a storm of protest from
some of these friends who recognised features of their characters and, in
particular, the celebrated landscape painter Levitan, who saw himself as
a model for Olga's lover.

Chekhov regarded the achievements of science as much more exciting
and important than the pretensions of the artistic community even though
the latter included many of his friends.

> Science and technology,

he wrote to Suvorin,

> are now going through a period of greatness, but, as for us, this is
> a precarious, sour, dreary period, and we ourselves are sour and
> dreary.

'Us' here refers to the artists and, in particular, writers. Literature had lost both its sense of direction and its confidence and was suffering from a condition that he likened to sexual impotence.

> If you lift up the skirts of our muse all you will see is a flat area.[5]

Science, in contrast, knew where it was going and had the wherewithal to transform thousands of lives. There was no doubt about its potency. Its practitioners were, however, held in low repute and made to work in conditions in which their new-found knowledge could not bear fruit or were being corrupted by the social mores and expectations of the society that surrounded them.

---

[5] A. Chekhov. Letter to A.S. Suvorin. 25 November 1892.

CHAPTER VIII

Pulmonary Tuberculosis

Lying on his back in Professor Ostroumov's clinic in Moscow University Hospital, prohibited at first from speaking, and with an ice-pack on his chest, Chekhov must have had leisure to review the past history of his own illness. He had only slowly come to realise that it bore gravely on his future. The first discharge of blood from the lungs had occurred in 1884, thirteen years previously, and just after his qualification in this very institution. He had been attending the Moscow District court as a part-time reporter. The case had been one of embezzlement affecting an employee of the Skopinsky bank.[1] Suddenly he was aware that blood was pouring into his mouth, and it seemed to be coming from his right lung every time that he coughed. It continued off and on for four days. He did not seek further advice but he must have realised at once that such a symptom could have a very serious significance. There was known tuberculosis in his family. Elizabeth, the daughter of his uncle Michael Michaelovitch had died from it at the age of twenty-six. When he was fifteen he had an episode of abdominal illness that had been labelled 'peritonitis' and since that time he had been troubled with recurring attacks of diarrhoea. Whether this was tuberculous enteritis must remain a real possibility.[2] However Chekhov was not anxious to face such possibilities and despite frequent attacks of coughing and bringing up blood during the next few years he feared putting any suspicions to the test. Writing to his friend Leiken in 1886 he expressed it frankly enough.

> I am afraid of being auscultated (examined by a stethoscope) by my colleagues. What if they find prolonged expiratory sounds, or

---

[1] A. Chekhov. Letter to N.A. Leykin. 10 December 1884.

[2] E.B. Meve. *op.cit.* Chapter 4.

bronchial breathing. It seems not to be the lungs that are at fault
but the throat.[3]

Such changes would have signalled consolidated lungs and certain
TB. In 1888 he wrote to Suvorin,

> I noticed a couple of times a year that I was bringing up blood,
> sometimes in large quantities so that I could taste it the whole time
> and sometimes more slightly. Each winter, autumn, spring and
> especially when the weather is humid I cough. But all this only
> frightens me when I see blood. There is something very ominous
> in the slow trickle of blood from the mouth, seen in the glow from
> the fire. But when there is no blood I am not worried and do not
> threaten literature with 'yet one more loss'. In fact consumption
> or any other lung disease can be recognised only through an
> aggregation of symptoms, and in my case there is not an aggregate.
> Expectoration in itself is not serious.   Sometimes a lung
> haemorrhage can go on for a whole day.... but the result is the
> patient goes on living, and this happens in the majority of patients.
> If the haemorrhage I had in the district court had been the
> beginning of consumption I should have been in the other world
> a long time ago. This is my kind of logic.[4]

So he tried to talk himself into ignoring the signs of disease that he
would immediately have recognised in a patient. Of course, before the
discovery of X-rays the clinical diagnosis of pulmonary tuberculosis was
much more difficult to make. The definitive test was to find tubercle
baccilli in the sputum. Ludwig Koch's paper describing his discovery
had only been published a few years previously in 1882.

Then another member of the family fell ill and in a way that was
impossible to ignore. Anton's younger brother Nicholas, who was an
artist working in Moscow and who had had persistent coughing for a few
years suddenly became acutely ill and Chekhov took him into his house
to care for him. On March 25th 1889 the doctor reports Nicholas as
having

> typhoid fever in a comparatively slight degree.

---

[3] A. Chekhov. Letter to N.A. Leykin. 6 April 1886.
[4] A. Chekhov. Letter to A.S. Suvorin. 14 October 1888.

This rather curious description suggests perhaps a persistently raised temperature. By March 29th Chekhov asked one of the consultant physicians, Dr Obolonsky, to visit his brother who was ill with 'pneumonia crouposa' which suggests that there was some obstruction to breathing in the larynx.[5] He added that he had arranged for eight dry cupping glasses to be put on and a warming poultice to be applied. Signs soon appeared at the apex of the lung.

> The temperature became hectic which always worries me when I have a patient with my brother's constitution. There is a flattening of the right apex above and below the clavicle. Crepitations are heard in two places which is where the nests of germs are and there is loss of weight.[6]

His brother's health does not seem to have improved and by May the diagnosis, perhaps made clear by Dr Obolonsky, is so definite that Chekhov can inform the older brother Alexander

> He has chronic lung consumption which is an incurable illness. During that illness there are temporary turns for the better, relapses and then maintenance of the status quo and the following question must arise. 'How long will the process last?' and not the question 'when is he going to recover?'.[7]

On June 4th he wrote again to Obolonsky

> The painter's affairs are going badly. The temperature is keeping up. His weight drops day by day. Since May, whenever he lies down it brings on the coughing. I give him quinine, atropine, etc.[8]

Despite everything his condition continued to deteriorate and he died on 17 June.

Watching his brother die from tuberculosis must have been both distressing and disturbing for the young doctor who was now showing unmistakable signs of the same disease. He confided to Obolonsky that he

---

[5] A. Chekhov. Letter to N.N. Obolonsky. 29 March 1889.
[6] A. Chekhov. Letter to N.A. Leykin. 10 April 1889.
[7] A. Chekhov. Letter to Alexander Chekhov. 8 May 1889.
[8] A. Chekhov. Letter to N.N. Obolonsky. 4 June 1889.

suffered from 'not influenza but some other swinishness'. Perhaps it was partly to expunge such fears and portents from his mind, or because of a growing conviction that his time for living was likely to be short, that he planned and executed his visit to Sakhalin in 1890. By this time it is clear that he had an active infection in both lungs and the rigours of the trans-Siberian journey together with the gruelling schedule of visits in the semi arctic conditions of Sakhalin must surely have sealed his fate. This was the view of his friend Rossolimo who qualified in Chekhov's year who knew him intimately during this time.[9] His letters on the journey referred frequently to his poor health. Almost at the start of the journey we find him writing to his sister Marya

> as a result of all this stress or from continual bother with the suitcases - and perhaps from the farewell carousing in Moscow, I have been spitting up blood again in the mornings and this has plunged me into a state of despondency and brought on gloomy thoughts.[10]

On returning he noticed the deterioration.

> I looked like a drowned man. My flu continues. I cannot stop coughing. Today I still have terrible headaches. I'm getting old. I haven't reached that age yet. Actually I'm on the way to something worse.

He at last acknowledges to Suvorin:

> I am already beginning to think that my health will never return to its former condition.[11]

But, despite these accurate intimations of what the true state of affairs was, he was reluctant to take the irrevocable step of putting himself in the hands of his own profession.

> Treatment and the care of one's physical existence inspires me with something approaching disgust. I am not going to have any

---

[9] G. Rossolimo. *Personal Reminiscences about Chekhov. The Russian Doctor.* 51. 1904. 1732-33.

[10] A. Chekhov. Letter to Marya Chekhov. April 1900.

[11] A. Chekhov. Letter to A.S. Suvorin. 13 November 1891.

treatment. I shall drink mineral waters and quinine, but I shall not allow myself to be examined.

Only someone with little experience of sick doctors would be surprised to find such an attitude in someone whose chosen pursuit is the treatment of illness. There is a great, almost impassible gulf between being in professional charge of illness and being a patient. In part this is due to knowing the limits as well as the advantages of treatment, but perhaps even more to an unwillingness to relinquish control over the management of one's everyday life to others.

The days and nights of exhausting work at Melikhova were punctuated by further attacks of illness.

> For a whole month the influenza has wasted my strength

he wrote to Natalya Lintvaryova December 1891:

> It first struck in the head and legs so that I had to lie in bed. And then it attacked my lungs so that I coughed frantically and became thin like a trail of smoke from a shot fired. What a pity! I've been at home without going outside at all for a whole month, lying down or walking about and with work up to my ears.[12]

He usually called his illness 'influenza' to try to disguise its true nature. He tried to reassure Suvorin: 'Coughing has increased' on November 11th 1893, 'but I think that consumption is still far away,'[13] and in February 1894: 'My cough gets me down, especially at sunrise, however there is nothing serious yet.'[14]

Did he know all the time and refused to acknowledge it to his friends, or was he deceiving himself? It was probably a bit of both. According to his brother Michael, to whom he wrote from his hospital bed, Chekhov showed surprise.

> How could I have not noticed this about myself before? Every year in March I have been spitting up blood but this year the expectoration was prolonged and I had to be admitted. Here, the followers of

---

[12] A. Chekhov. Letter to N. Lintvaryova. 14 December 1891.
[13] A. Chekhov. Letter to A.S. Suvorin. 11 November 1893.
[14] A. Chekhov. Letter to A.S. Suvorin. February 1894.

Aesculapius enlightened my blissful ignorance and found some infected sputum in the apex of each lung.[15]

The medical notes recorded his exhausted appearance and his long but narrow chest. His weight, 62 kg was small for his 1.86 metres height. He was pale, cold and sweating. Examination of the chest showed moist sounds on both sides above and below the clavicle. As Chekhov had mentioned, tubercle baccilli were discovered in his sputum.[16]

After the first few days his symptoms had subsided to some extent and restrictions on his activities were lessened. Visitors were allowed although they were confined to a few minutes and asked not to exhaust him. Suvorin found him sitting up in bed laughing and joking as usual with a large glass of blood stained sputum by his side.

To calm patients

he said

we say when they have a cough it is gastric and when they have a haemorrhage it is a burst vein. But gastric coughs do not exist and coughed up blood definitely comes from the lungs. Blood is coming from my right lung as it did in the case of my brother, and another of my tuberculous relatives. The doctors try and tell me, as a doctor, that it is a gastric haemorrhage. I listen to them but don't take any notice; I know I have TB.

When Suvorin told him that he had been watching the ice breaking up and moving on the Moscva river he suddenly changed his expression and said: 'Really, is the river moving? I wish I had thought about that.'[17] He connected the melting of the river with his renewed bleeding, which seems to be derived from some old tale relating the seasons and bodily disease.

Another distinguished visitor that he was pleased, even proud, to see was Tolstoy.

It's an ill wind that doesn't blow some good

---

[15] V.V. Khizniakov. *op.cit.* p.49.
[16] E.B. Meve. *op.cit.* Chapter 4.
[17] A. S. Suvorin. Diary 1923. pp.150-151.

he wrote later.

> Tolstoy came to see me and we had a most interesting conversation.
> Interesting mainly for me because I listened more than I talked.
> We discussed immortality. He recognises immortality in its
> Kantian form, assuming that all of us, men and animals, will live
> on embodied in some principle, reason or love, the essence of
> which is a mystery. But I can only imagine such a principle or
> force as a shapeless, gelatinous mass. My 'I', my individuality, my
> consciousness would merge with this mass. I feel no need for this
> sort of immortality. I do not understand it and Lev Nicolayavitch
> was astounded that I didn't.[18]

He described to Chekhov the vast reading that he had been doing for
his essay 'What is art?' and outlined his argument which Chekhov
immediately found unacceptable. Then, having overstayed his alloted
time by at least half an hour he left the room. The invalid had another
violent haemorrhage during the night.

As soon as he was able to write he sent a letter to the school-teacher
who was engaged for the latest of his village schools at Novosyolki.

> Come and visit the sick. They don't let anyone in but they'll let you
> if you insist and show this note which I enclose.[19]

He was worried about the schoolmaster's house and about the
progress of the school building which he was supposed to be supervising.
As more and more of his acquaintances heard of his confinement the
stream of visitors to the hospital steadily increased. They were welcome
at first but later on it became too much of a good thing.

> Yesterday I had visitors all day

he wrote to Suvorin on April 7th.

> It was simply disastrous. They were allowed in two at a time. They
> first said I should not talk and then kept asking me questions..... I

---

[18] A. Chekhov. Letter to M. Menshikov. 16th April 1897.
[19] A. Chekhov. Letter to N.J. Zubarin. 27 March 1897.

must get married. An ill-natured wife might perhaps be able to reduce my visitors by half.[20]

His correspondence was also a big burden, replying to all the letters of sympathy, and reading stories sent to him by aspiring young authors, replying with encouragement and criticism on matters of style.

If the diagnosis was now established there was still plenty of argument about what should be done about it.

> The doctors have diagnosed pulmonary apical lesions and ordered me to change my way of life. I can understand the former but not the latter because it is almost impossible. They order me to live in the country, but living permanently in the country presupposes constantly fussing round with peasants, animals and the elements in all their forms, and it is as difficult to avoid cares and anxieties in the country as it is burns in hell. But I will still try and change my life as much as possible, and I've already sent word to Marya that I will no longer practice medicine in the country. It will be both a relief and a great deprivation for me. I am giving up all my district duties and buying a dressing gown and I will bask in the sun and eat and eat. My doctors have told me to eat about six times a day and they are indignant at finding that I eat so little. I am forbidden to do much talking or go swimming and so on. All my organs other than the lungs are found to be healthy. Until now I felt as if I had been drinking as much as I could without doing any harm to myself but it turns out I have been drinking less than I was entitled to. What a pity![21]

The accepted treatment for pulmonary tuberculosis was then to encourage the patient to eat as many meals as possible with a high fat content to the food in an attempt to prevent the wasting that was regarded as an ominous sign. In summer there was strict confinement to the bedroom with avoidance of direct sunlight and fresh air, and during the winter, for those who could afford it, a journey to the south, Sochi, Yalta or the French Riviera. Chekhov, always abstemious about food, disliked the overfeeding.

---

[20] A. Chekhov. Letter to A.S. Suvorin. 7 April 1897.
[21] A. Chekhov. Letter to A.S. Suvorin. 1 April 1897.

They make me eat enormously. My belly is stuffed. Ferocious
overfeeding,

he complains to Suvorin.

If the experiments with Koch's new preparation produces
favourable results, I shall take a trip to Berlin of course. Eating is
doing me absolutely no good. They have been cramming me with
food for the last two weeks but it is of little use. There is no increase
in weight.[22]

He wrote to Alexander saying that they would be releasing him on
Wednesday of Passion week but warning him not to let his mother and
father know the real nature of his illness. His youngest brother Ivan
accompanied him home and they stopped on the way to inspect the new
school at Novosyolki. Once at Melikhova, although he did not resume
his regular medical practice there was a continuous round of other duties.
Funds for the new school had to be found. There were plans for a
psychiatric unit for alcoholics and even an appeal to the ecclesiastical
authorities to return a well-loved local priest who had been moved from
Serpukhov. But Chekhov's store of energy was not what it had been.
Jean Schleglov, a friend who came to pay a visit was shocked at the
change.

His face was yellow and he looked worn out. He coughed frequently
and wrapped himself in his blanket as if cold although the wind
was inexplicably warm.
Do you know, Jean, what I need now? A year's holiday, neither
more nor less - but a real rest you understand. One year to catch
my breath and then I'll work like a black.[23]

Meanwhile, visitors started pouring in and were always received with
a welcome though some stayed for days or even weeks. By July, he was
writing

I have enough house guests to fill a pond. I am out of space, out
of bedding, and out of patience talking with them all.

---

[22] A. Chekhov. Letter to A.S. Suvorin. 7 April 1897.
[23] J. Schleglov. *A.P. Chekhov, his literary customs and his work.* 1928. p.285.

Perhaps it was just as well that the doctors at the hospital had given him strict instructions to go before the onset of winter, either to the Crimea or the Riviera. He decided on Nice and, leaving Russia on September 1st he went through to Biarritz where he stayed for a few days before travelling to Nice and putting up at a quiet hotel away from the waterfront, called the Pension Russe. There was a small colony of Russians in this part of the town, some who had escaped for political reasons and others in search of health. The Pension Russe catered particularly for them and had a Russian proprietress and, more advantageously, a Russian chef. Chekhov made quick friends with several of his countrymen, particularly one Maxim Kovalevski, a former Moscow professor of history, who had been dismissed from the University for political subversion and had decided to live abroad. He subsequently started a Russian school of sociology in Paris. They both found a similar sense of humour and spent their mealtimes denouncing with gusto members of the Russian literary establishment. Kovalevski said that Chekhov had explained to him that he could not undertake any lengthy work because, as a doctor, he knew that his life would be a short one.

Another neighbour in the Russian quarter turned out to be Nemirovitch Dashenko, the famous theatre director of the Moscow Arts Theatre, with whom Chekhov was to be closely associated in his last few years. He reported the following conversation with Chekhov about a painter called Yacobi, who was also suffering from TB.[24]

> 'Yacobi will die soon.'
> 'Why?'
> 'He wants to deceive himself. Look for yourself. He will tell anecdotes. He laughs. But in his eyes there is death. Yes. In any case we are all sentenced.'
> 'From birth?'
> 'No. I'm talking of myself. And yet you know I so much want to live, to write more. It's hard to be a doctor you know. You exaggerate everything.'

More macabrely he told Nemirovitch Dashenko that he had just been up the coast to Menton where he had seen rows of tuberculosis patients lined up on the beach in their chairs, spitting. The sea, healthy, calm and

---

[24] E.B. Meve. *op.cit*. Chapter 4.

brave rolled towards them. Near the chairs stood the wives and husbands of the sick patients. He would like to write a story he said, about how these relatives feel, like slaves chained to the galleys. And nature does not care about themselves or their charges.

At first his health improved but by November 10th the spitting of blood started again and continued for three weeks.

> I don't leave the house until three o'clock in the afternoon and when I do it's only to walk along the street. I don't drink anything, don't eat hot foods, don't walk fast. In short I'm not living but vegetating. This irritates me. I'm in a bad temper. It always seems to me at dinner that the Russians are making stupid and vulgar remarks and I have to force myself not to speak to them impertinently. But for God's sake don't tell anyone about the blood spitting. This is confidential. I write home that all is well with me and it's not sensible to say anything different. I really do feel fine and if they find out at home that I have haemorrhages they will set up such a wail.[25]

By the spring he was feeling better and took a great interest in the Dreyfus case that was then the talk of everybody in France and dividing conservative from radical opinion. Chekhov greatly admired Zola's stand and knew that the French government must sooner or later climb down, but found to his dismay that Suvorin's newspaper which was well known for its conservative views took the opposite position. He immediately wrote to his friend dissenting strongly from his paper's stand. Before returning home he bought 319 volumes of French classics for the library at his birthplace Taganrog and had them parcelled up and dispatched. 'They cost me a lot of money and I'm afraid the censor will delay them or perhaps even confiscate half of them.'

Back at Melikhova he supervised the completion of his third school before travelling south to the Black Sea coast. Whilst he was there he heard that his father had died suddenly and decided that the time had come to look for a permanent house in the south to move into with his sister and mother. A piece of land was found a few miles from the centre of Yalta next to a Tartar colony. It was gently sloping ground on which Chekhov designed and built his last house with an enormous balcony

---

[25] A. Chekhov. Letter to A.L. Suvorina. 10 November 1897.

Chekhov's house in Yalta.

over the front porch and an extensive garden with box hedges, palm trees, flower beds and an orchard which is still to be seen, very much as he left it but, when I was there, overgrown with trees. Melikhova was put on the market and he was joined by his family.

Any thought that this was to be a haven of rest for him was soon dispelled. Once the building of the house had been completed he turned his attention at once to the medical problems of Yalta, in particular the large number of consumptives that inundated the resort each year. He became an active member of the committee that arranged for reception of the sick and supervision of their care.

These sick people will be the death of me

he wrote to his brother Michael.

> They have been sent here from all over Russia with their bacilli, their lungs full of cavities, with livid complexions and without a penny in their pockets. They have to struggle with this nightmare trying all sorts of tricks just to survive.[26]

To Maxim Gorki who was then starting to make a literary career for himself and who had become very attached to Chekhov he complained of the senseless policy that was being followed.

> You should see their faces when they beg for help and you should see those pitiful blankets when they die. Your doctors up there in the north send tubercular cases here because they are ignorant of local conditions. If they are only incipient cases then there is some sense in sending them here for the autumn and winter. But to send terminal cases here, even in the summer months when it's as hot and oppressive here as in an oven, and in Russia it is pleasant, that is utterly wrong.[27]

One thing that was badly needed was the provision of more accommodation and Chekhov immediately started a fund to finance the building of a sanatorium. Soon the plans were made and building started.

---

[26] V.V. Khizniakov. *op.cit.*
[27] V.V. Khizniakov. *op.cit.*

If he wasn't engaged in the sanitorium he would be attending the meetings of a committee to commemorate the birth of Pushkin, acting as honorary superintendent of a girls school or raising more money, this time for famine relief in the Province of Samara.

The difficult task of restraining him fell to his personal doctor throughout his years in Yalta, Altschuller, who left an account of his difficulties with this wayward patient.[28] He was very insistent that Chekhov did not travel north in the winter months. These were the days when he was writing *Three Sisters* and *The Cherry Orchard* which were receiving their first performances by the Moscow Arts Theatre. As well as taking an interest in the productions he was rapidly falling in love with one of the principal actresses, Olga Knipper. It was practically impossible to persuade him to remain away from Moscow in these circumstances and there was much bargaining between doctor and patient. Meanwhile the infection in the lungs continued to spread. On one of his Moscow visits in March 1900 he was seen at the hospital by a Dr Schurovsky who

> found a great deterioration in me. Previously only the apices of the lungs were dull. Now this has extended in the front below the collar bone and, at the back, half way down the shoulder blades.[29]

There were few days now that were free from trouble.

> I received your letter

he replied to a friend in 1901

> lying on my back in the middle of a haemorrhage. No sooner do I arrive in Yalta but everything happens. It is either coughing or intestinal trouble or this thing nearly every day,[30]

and to another,

> I'm unwell, or to be entirely accurate, I am not entirely well and find it impossible to write. I've been spitting up blood and I feel

---

[28] I. Altschuller. Extracts from *Reminiscences about A P Chekhov. Russian News*. 1914. No. 151. p.3.
[29] V.V. Khizniakov. *op.cit.* p.49.
[30] A. Chekhov. Letter to N Kondakov. December 1901.

weak and cross. I've got a hot compress on my side and I'm taking creosote and all kinds of nonsense.[31]

Meanwhile, Chekhov's romance with Olga had been growing rapidly. Early in 1901 he had asked her if she would marry him.

> If you will give me your word that not a soul in Moscow will know of our wedding until after the day itself, I will make it the day after my arrival if you want. For some reason I'm frightened of all that wedding ceremony and the congratulations and the glass of champagne that you have to hold, with a vague smile on your face.[32]

On May 25th they were married in the little Church of the Holy Cross in Moscow with no one present but the four witnesses that were required by law and, once the ceremony was over, Chekhov immediately wrote to his sister Marya who until then had looked after him and the family, explaining what he had done. Then the pair set out on a strange honeymoon, at first to Nizhni Novgorod and then to Aksyonovo in Ufa Province to try a kumis cure. Whether this was Schurovsky's idea or Olga's it is difficult to be sure. It is not likely to be Chekhov's as he seems to have had little confidence in it. Kumis is made by fermenting mare's milk in old leather sacks and is a traditional drink of the Tartars and Baskars in this part of Russia. It had acquired a reputation of being able to cure pulmonary tuberculosis. The patient was expected to live with the tribe for several months, drinking from six to eight bottles of the kumis each day. When they arrived they received a letter from Marya that must have crossed his, which advised her brother strongly not to get married. He sat down straight away and replied that the marriage would not alter his close relationship with Marya and invited her, if she wished, to come and join Olga and himself. He would not be staying long because

> this place is horribly boring, the newspapers are years out of date and the other patients are very stodgy, Baskars all over the place and I would not stay here a minute if it were not for fishing and writing letters.[33]

---

[31] A. Chekhov. Letter to V.S. Mirolyubov. 17 December 1901.
[32] A. Chekhov. Letter to O. Knipper. 26 April 1901.
[33] A. Chekhov. Letter to Marya Chekhov. 4 June 1901.

However he said that he did feel a bit better and had put on eight pounds in weight though whether it was due to kumis or marriage he had no idea.Some time previously Chekhov had explained to Suvorin that if he ever married he could never set up house all the time with his wife, that she would have to come and go like the moon. This exactly describes the strange partnership that now prevailed, Olga continuing through the season with her work on the stage in Moscow whilst Chekhov stayed at Yalta, writing frequent letters, and when he found the strength continuing with his plays and stories.

August 29th, 1902.

> My dear wife, my actress, my hound, greetings!..... who wrote to you that I am so comfortable here? Why do you ask me what Altschuller told me? This doctor often drops in to see me. He wanted to listen to my chest. He insisted on it. But I refused. My mood? Excellent. My health? Yesterday I felt awful and took some humyadi but today I feel much better. As usual I cough more than when I was in the north.[34]

September 20th.

> Altschuller will come tomorrow. He will listen to my chest for the first time this autumn. I have kept putting him off but I can't do it any longer. He keeps trying to frighten me, saying that he will write to you. Here in Yalta everyone seems to think you are a virago and that you keep me under your thumb.[35]

September 22nd.

> Altschuller came yesterday and for the first time examined me. He listened to me, tapped me all over and found my heart had greatly improved to judge by the change that has come over me since spring. I seem to be getting free from disease.

He must have known that such a statement was probably untrue. Perhaps he was just reassuring Olga.

PHOTO LEFT
*Chekhov and
his wife, Olga.*

[34] A. Chekhov. Letter to O. Knipper. 29 August 1902.
[35] A. Chekhov. Letter to O. Knipper. 20 September 1902.

At any rate he has given me permission to visit Moscow. That's splendid. I mustn't go immediately but wait for the first frosts. So you see! He puts down my improvement to the creosote and to the fact that I have stayed in Yalta during the winter. Altschuller insists that I must leave Moscow as soon as I get there. I have said I will leave in December when my wife lets me.[36]

January 13th, 1903.

On the morning of the 11th after Marya had left town I didn't feel very well. I had a pain in my chest. I felt nauseated. I had a temperature of 38°C and yesterday it was also raised. I slept fairly well though my sleep was disturbed by pain. Altschuller looked in. He asked for a compress to be put on. An enormous one. This morning my temperature was down to 37°C. I feel weak and will have to put on that compress directly. However, I'm allowed to telegraph you that all is well. I'm improving. By tomorrow I shall be much better. I'm not hiding anything from you. Do realise that, and don't upset yourself by telegraphing me. If anything serious, or even resembling anything serious should happen, you should be the first I should tell.[37]

February 22nd, 1903.

My little grey puppy! Greetings! Yes, there you are getting flowers from Yermolova whilst I sit unwashed like a samoyed. I even begin to growl. You ask me if I at least wash my neck. Yes, I wash my neck but the rest of me is as dirty as an old galosh. I want to go to the bath-house but Altschuller will not let me.[38]

In May and June, much against Altschuller's advice, Chekhov went travelling again in Russia and then called in to see Professor Ostroumov once more.

He gave me a complete examination and said that my right lung was in a very bad state. He also found emphysema, and the

---

[36] A. Chekhov. Letter to O. Knipper. 22 September 1902.
[37] A. Chekhov. Letter to O. Knipper. January 13 1903.
[38] A. Chekhov. Letter to O. Knipper. February 22 1903.

remains of pleurisy. He told me off. 'You're a cripple,' he said and ordered me to spend the winter in the north near Moscow and not in the Crimea.[39]

When medical conditions are desperate the authorities often disagree. But the patient was beginning to lose his optimism, understandably. Maxim Gorki, visiting him at his Yalta house, found him

> lying on the sofa coughing his dry cough and playing with his thermometer.

He greeted him with -

> to live in order to die is not amusing, but to live knowing that one must die prematurely is absolutely stupid.[40]

Altschuller found him less and less in a good humour and often sitting alone in an armchair or reclining with his eyes shut and without the usual book in his hands.

A young student, Tikhonov, visited him and described seeing him

> coming down the garden, walking carefully, a big round shouldered man, his face with a pointed greying beard was grey with fatigue. At his left hand side hung a bottle in a leather case of the kind that hunters wear. His crumpled enormous trousers flapped round his long legs, whose knees touched. A few paces from us a long spasm of coughing gripped him. Unscrewing the top of his bottle and turning away with embarrassment he spat into the bottle a thick red fluid, then pressed my hand with his clammy one without speaking.[41]

He was completing his last play *The Cherry Orchard* and a few more stories, but they cost him painful efforts. Often he had to take to his bed after completing half a page.

The last two stories *The Bishop* and *A Marriageable Girl*, both concern death. The first is an account of the death of a bishop from typhoid fever.

[39] A. Chekhov. Letter to A.S. Suvorin. 17 June 1903.
[40] V.V. Khizniakov. *op.cit.* p.51.
[41] V. Tikhonov. *Anton P. Chekhov. Reminiscences and Letters in About Chekhov. Reminiscences and Articles.* Moscow 1910. p.219-241.

Walking the dog in the Yalta garden.

He is taken suddenly ill whilst celebrating the Easter services. Chekhov contrasts the jewelled magnificence of the ceremonies and the eternal symbolism with the frailty of the human being in one of his masterpieces. Although he had early abandoned the orthodox faith of his boyhood he retained an affection for the beautiful ceremonies of the eastern rite. *A Marriageable Girl* is not quite in the same class but Chekhov's situation is reflected in the illness of the architect Sasha, who has tuberculosis. He is instrumental in liberating the girl Nadia from a planned marriage to the son of the local priest and a future of provincial boredom. She goes off to study in Petersburg but hears when she returns that Sasha has died from his TB in Saratov. *The Cherry Orchard* itself is very much a valedictory exercise, full of farewells, to the old Russia, to a whole generation of a family and to the beloved orchard.

Stanislavsky who was supervising the rehearsals hoped that Chekhov would be able to attend the opening night which was to take place in January 1904. But the problems of getting him once more up to Moscow were daunting.

> I very much want to go to Moscow but I don't see how I can break away from here. It's growing cold and I almost never leave the house. I'm not used to being out of doors and coughing. It's not the trip itself that I'm worried about but the change over at Sevastapol that lasts from two o'clock until eight.[42]

Despite these misgivings he was present at the Moscow Arts Theatre on 17th January for the first performance. What he had not been told was that a great public ceremony had been prepared to commemorate the 25th anniversary of his literary debut. After the third act he was invited onto the stage and treated to long and fulsome speeches from all kinds of dignitaries. They had not reckoned on him being as seriously ill as he now appeared. Stanislavsky, looking back, said later

> when, after the third act, he approached the stage, deathly pale and thin and unable to stop coughing during his welcome with speeches and presents, our hearts were heavy.[43]

No one doubted now that the end was not far off.

---

[42] A. Chekhov. Letter to K.S. Slanislavksy. 30 October 1903.
[43] K.S. Stanislavsky. *Moya zhizn v iskusstve*. Moscow. 1941.

Olga stayed in Moscow for a month or so to finish the season. Back
in Yalta Chekhov wrote to her in March:

> My dear remarkable little half, I am alive, strong as a bull, in good
> spirits and there is only one thing I can't get used to. My monkish
> state. I have a favour to ask you my darling. As you know I am
> a physician and a friend of the Women's Medical School. When
> *The Cherry Orchard* was announced the students asked me as a
> doctor to arrange a performance of the play for the benefit of the
> women students. They are terribly poor. Many of them are
> expelled for failing to pay their tuition fees etc. I said I would take
> up the matter with the director and did so obtaining a promise to
> co-operate. Before I left Moscow Nemirovitch told me that it
> would hardly be possible to arrange the benefit in St Petersburg at
> the moment. 'It is wartime and the takings would be almost nil.
> Would it not be better to arrange a literary matinée for the students
> benefit?' So, my dear one, do remind him now and insist that the
> matinée takes place.[44]

To the end of his life the appeals on behalf of the organisations and
individuals in need never stopped, but this was to be the last. With the
season over, Olga joined him and they decided to travel to Germany to
consult another specialist in Berlin before going on to the spa town of
Badenweiler. He wrote to Marya from Berlin on June 6th,

> I've been here a whole day now. It turned very cold in Moscow
> and even snowed after you left. The bad weather must have given
> me a cold. My legs have begun to ache. I had not slept for nights
> and lost much weight. I have given myself injections of morphine
> and taken thousands of medicines. The only thing that did me any
> good was the heroin for which Altschuller had given me a
> prescription. However, before I left I had started to pick up and
> finally left the country looking very thin with thin and skinny legs.
> I had a good journey. Here in Berlin we have taken a good room
> in the best hotel. I'm very much enjoying the life and haven't eaten
> so well for a long time..... I'm already putting on weight and today,
> despite the cold weather, I even took a ride to the Tiergarten. And

---

[44] A. Chekhov. Letter to O. Knipper. 3 March 1904.

The health resort of Badenweiler where Chekhov died on 15th July, 1904.

so you can tell mother and everyone else who is interested that I'm
on my way to recovery, or even that I have already recovered. My
legs no longer ache. I have no more diarrhoea. I'm beginning to
grow fat and now I spend my whole day on my feet - out of bed.
Tomorrow I will be visited by a local celebrity Professor Ewald,
an internal specialist. Dr Taube wrote to him concerning me.[45]

Chekhov gives no hint of what Professor Ewald thought. No doubt
he found something tactful to say to the dying Russian writer. To nearly
all his correspondents Chekhov wrote to explain that he was making a
marvellous recovery. Most of this was probably designed to spare his
family and friends from distress on his behalf but was he also, as he had
before, trying to talk his way into optimism? Olga described him sitting
in the little guest room in which they stayed at Badenweiler, choking with
emphysema and surrounded by travel guides. He intended to return to
Russia soon, but not by the shortest and most convenient route. He
thought he would travel through Italy. When she was asked whether he
often entertained thoughts of death she said that he did but that such
thoughts were not permanently in his mind and right up to the end of his

---

[45] A. Chekhov. Letter to Marya Chekhov. 6 June 1904.

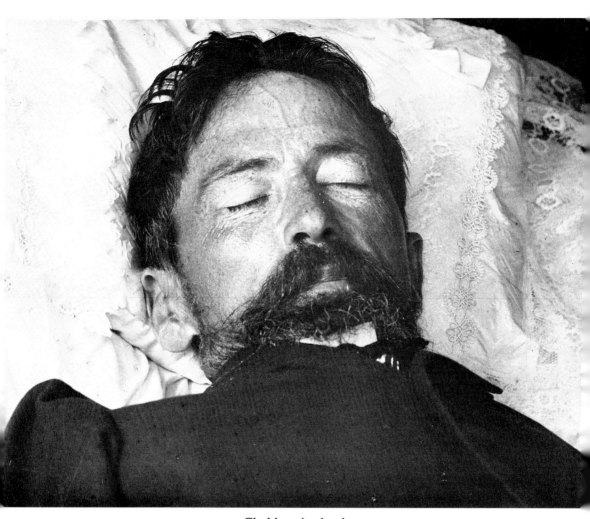

Chekhov in death.

life he behaved as one who is sure of his tomorrow. On the other hand three days before he died he spoke of the necessity of transferring to Olga's name a sum of money that was in his name in the local bank. He was well aware that there was a point at which the fantasy had to stop.

The weather was very hot and, with the trip home in mind, he sent Olga to Freiburg to get him a light flannel suit. On June 28th he wrote to Marya for the last time asking for details of a travel itinerary for the journey home. For once he confessed that all was not well with his health.

I eat delicious food but very little of it for my stomach is repeatedly upset. I may not eat butter here. Obviously my stomach is in a hopeless condition and there is no other remedy than fasting, ie, to stop eating entirely - and that's final. Basta! As for my shortness of breath the only remedy is not to move.[46]

The last letter was written on the same day to his old friend Rossolimo who had been with him in medical school and was now teaching in Moscow.

I have had a high temperature every day.... my breathing is laboured enough to make you want to scream and there are even moments when I quite lose heart.[47]

Dr Schwerer who visited him from the town happened to have a Russian wife. He paid frequent calls on the guest house.

On Tuesday

(June 29th) he wrote later

the state of Chekhov's heart did not give rise to serious worry. But on the night from Thursday to Friday when the pulse did not react after the first camphor injection it became evident that the end was near! Chekhov was awake soon after midnight and became delirious. He kept on talking about some sailor and was asking about the Japanese. But then he came to and with a sad smile said to his wife, who was placing some ice on his chest 'no one puts ice on an empty heart.'[48]

Olga described the last hours on July 15th.

At the beginning of the night Anton Pavlovitch woke up and, for the first time in his life, asked himself for the doctor to be fetched. The doctor came and asked for some champagne to be given to the

---

[46] A. Chekhov. Letter to Marya Chekhov. 28 June 1904.

[47] A. Chekhov. Letter to G. Rossolimo. 28 June 1904.

[48] G.B. Iollos and O.L. Knipper. *A.P. Chekhov. Lyturaturni byt y tvochestvo po mennarnym materialam*. Leningrad 1928. pp.455-6.

The funeral procession approaches Kuzetsky Bridge.

patient. Anton Pavlovitch sat up and with great deliberation said to the doctor 'Ich sterbe.' Then he took the glass, turned his face towards me, smiled his extraordinary smile and said, 'It's a long time since I drank champagne', quietly drank up to the dregs, lay down silently on his left side and was soon still for ever.[49]

The body was brought back to Russia in a refrigerated railway car bearing the Chekhovian inscription 'for oysters'. Large crowds gathered for the funeral at the Novadevichy cemetary in Moscow. Among the mourners were Maxim Gorki and Fyodor Chaliapin. Olga and Marya grew to be close friends and lived until the nineteen thirties corresponding frequently and sharing their memories of the remarkable human being who had claimed so much of their affection.

---

[49] O. Knipper Chekhova. *Afterwords about A.P. Chekhov*. Slovo. Berlin. 1924.